DESCENT

DESCENT

LAUREN RUSSELL

Tarpaulin Sky Press
Saxtons River, VT
2020

Descent
© 2020 Lauren Russell
ISBN-13: 978-1-939460-21-9
Printed and bound in the USA

Cover art by Sarah Stefana Smith.
Mend (2018) from series *A/mends*.
Materials: Black bird netting, Fishing line, and Black thread.
Dimensions: 75 x 15 x 14 inches.

Tarpaulin Sky Press
P.O. Box 189
Grafton, Vermont 05146
TarpaulinSky.com

For more information on Tarpaulin Sky Press trade paperback and hand-bound
editions, as well as information regarding distribution, personal orders, and catalogue
requests, please visit our website at tarpaulinsky.com.

for Kian and Roya

It matters that there are holes in a family history that can never be filled, that there are secrets and mysteries, migrations and invasions and murky blood-lines. These stories speak of human history.

—Eleni Sikelianos, from *The Book of Jon*

I was determined to fill in the blank spaces of the historical record and to represent the lives of those deemed unworthy of remembering, but how does one write a story about an encounter with nothing?

—Saidiya Hartman, from *Lose Your Mother*

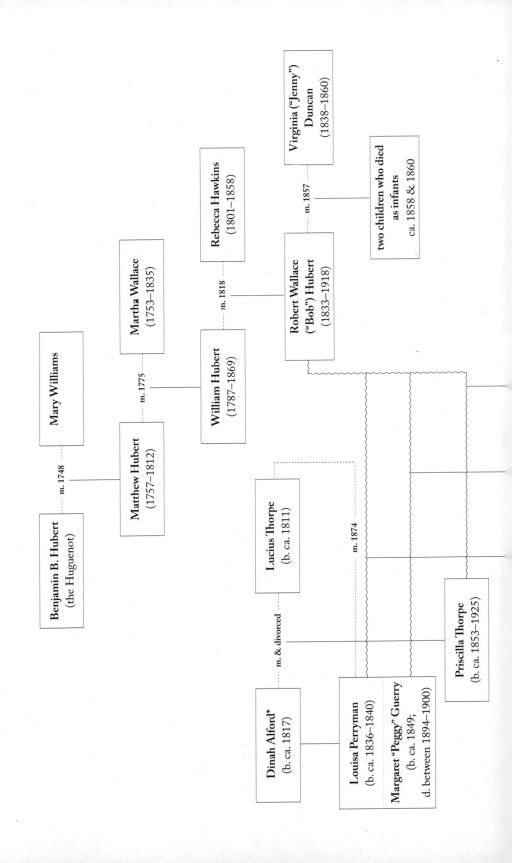

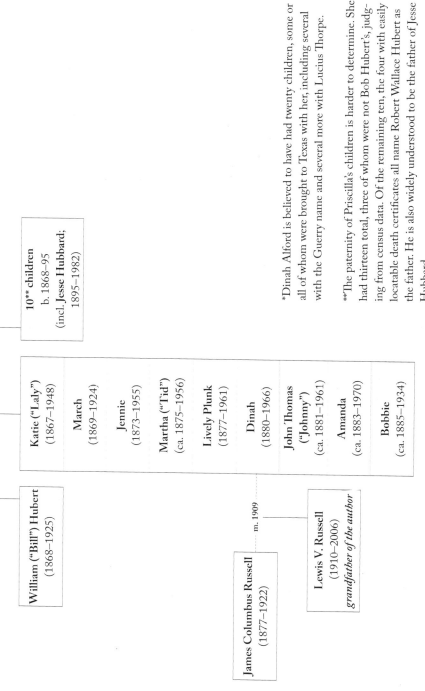

10 children**
b. 1868–95
(incl. **Jesse Hubbard**;
1895–1982)

William ("Bill") Hubert
(1868–1925)

Katie ("Laly")
(1867–1948)

March
(1869–1924)

Jennie
(1873–1955)

Martha ("Tid")
(ca. 1875–1956)

Lively Plunk
(1877–1961)

Dinah
(1880–1966)

John Thomas ("Johnny")
(ca. 1881–1961)

Amanda
(ca. 1883–1970)

Bobbie
(ca. 1885–1934)

m. 1909

James Columbus Russell
(1877–1922)

Lewis V. Russell
(1910–2006)
grandfather of the author

*Dinah Alford is believed to have had twenty children, some or all of whom were brought to Texas with her, including several with the Guerry name and several more with Lucius Thorpe.

**The paternity of Priscilla's children is harder to determine. She had thirteen total, three of whom were not Bob Hubert's, judging from census data. Of the remaining ten, the four with easily locatable death certificates all name Robert Wallace Hubert as the father. He is also widely understood to be the father of Jesse Hubbard.

W hat happened between or out of or in the holes of
the story is the real story. What cannot be filled
in with sod or whisked away with dust. Because history is
neither the truth as it happened nor necessarily the truth
we most want to believe. When I look at the family tree I
see so many faceless names skewered on ascending boughs,
making whole orchards of molding fruit, a hodgepodge of
known or estimated dates, origins, migration patterns. I
can imagine these known and unknown ancestors in grave-
yards reaching out across the oceans—to West African
villages where someone was kidnapped venturing too far
from the fold or was captured in a raid, enslaved, sold; to
the farms and teeming cities of Western Europe, where a
"heretic" fled for religious freedom, or a younger son got
dizzy on the rumor of fortune, or men and women left in
ones or twos or whole families trickling in on steerage, to
escape the farm, the shop, the lord. Most of their stories I
do not know—but I see these faceless, often nameless an-
cestors arriving at a harbor (Charleston? Baltimore? New
York?)—free and ecstatic or subdued by the prospect of
endless work, the unknown land; or staggering onto a deck
with shackles boring bloody welts into their skin, stunned
by the sudden light, their languages ricocheting off each
other, and when forced to bend to the master tongue, still

maintaining some of their posture. In the centuries that follow, occasionally someone leaves a diary full of holes, and you glimpse a personality, a record shaped, curated for "posterity." History belongs to the victor? Perhaps to the one with the loudest pen. (So forced illiteracy has historical ends.) Mythology grows in the distance between record and memory over several generations so that a farm becomes a great sawmill and a slave woman embarks on an unlikely thousand-mile journey (declining a chance at liberty) to visit her master, a Confederate prisoner of war, who promises a great reward.

What I know is this: Sometime before 1746, Benjamin Hubert, a French Huguenot, arrived in the "New World" with his desperation and his faith. But the path from persecuted to persecutor is as narrow as the slave trader's whip. In his will, recorded in Georgia in 1793, Hubert left his youngest son 100 acres, including a plantation, and "one Negro boy named Rob." By 1798, Benjamin Hubert's oldest son Matthew owned six slaves. Half a century later, Matthew's son William was still in Georgia, the owner of a plantation and the fifty-six human beings whose labor supported it. William Hubert's daughter, Martha, had married J.A.S. Turner, a wealthy Georgian whose family's plantation, Turnwold, and its slave inhabitants, were the source of the Uncle Remus stories.

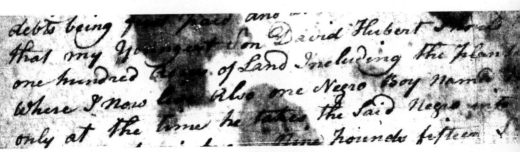

Courtesy of Washington Memorial Library in Macon, Georgia

Turner had taken a fancy to Texas as a Captain in the Mexican War, riding hard on the heels of Manifest Destiny. His own destiny manifested in the form of an exodus. When the Republic of Texas won independence from Mexico in 1836, it used land as currency to pay soldiers and encourage settlement, and after it was annexed to the United States in 1845, Texas continued to dole out land at about fifty cents an acre. By the mid-19th century, white settlers were invading the state like an Old Testament plague. But the Native inhabitants they drove away weren't headed for any land of Canaan. For decades the Alabama and Coushatta had been living in the Big Thicket of East Texas, and in 1853 the Alabama petitioned the Texas legislature for land as their position became increasingly precarious. The following year the State of Texas settled the tribe onto an eleven-hundred-acre reservation that became more crowded once the Coushatta arrived in 1859. That year the inhabitants of every other Texas reservation were banished to Indian Territory in what is now Oklahoma, opening the way for white settlement. By then the Turners had already headed West, and out of family feeling or an itch for land acquisition, the Huberts had decided to come along. Among the many human possessions they brought to Texas was the slave Dinah Alford, a mother of twenty. Three of Dinah's daughters—Margaret, called Peggy; Louisa; and Priscilla—would have children by one of the Hubert sons—Robert, called Bob—after his return from the Civil War. One of those children was my great-grandmother.

I am not writing a history of what happened, which I cannot know. I am writing into the silences, the omissions, what has been left out either intentionally or because by its nature it defies legibility. I am writing into the space where one story trails off and another begins, oddly muddled, or between what some might have thought and what they dared to utter, or beyond what no one was sure of but everybody recollected, or within what only I imagined, bent over a photocopy of a photocopy of my great-great-grandfather's diary and a stack of books and records, trying to fill in the letters between H and P. This is not a history or a fiction. I would like to invoke Audre Lorde's term "biomythography" and puncture its seams, pull out its hem, and make "biomythology" from the swaying threads. Thus there may be several versions of the same events. None may be true but all could have been—climbing a web of omission, legacy, myth.

Dear Robert, Dear Redbeard, Dear Specter of the Great White Father, Dear Slaveholder, Dear Confederate Captain Captured at Gettysburg, Dear Dispenser of Land Favors Semen, Procreator of Twenty Children by Three Sisters Simultaneously, Dear Father of the Negro League Pitcher, Dear Farmer Schoolmaster Landlord Hired Hand Grave Paler Log Roller Surveyor and Manure Shoveler, Dear Singer, Dear Churchman and Circus Fan, Dear Reveler at Brigade Reunions, Dear Collector of Sentimental Poems about Loneliness and Redemption, Dear Pointy Eared Like Lucifer and Bearded Beyond Rasputin, Dear Mythical Jim Crow Defier, Hero of my Grandfather's Childhood, Who Took Him on the "Whites Only" Section of the Streetcar (He Claimed This Really Happened) Proclaiming "These Are My Grandchildren & They're Sitting With Me!", Dear Diarist, Dear Widower, Dear Lonesome Hunger, Dear Admirer of Well-Formed Women, Dear Inscrutable in the Tintype Beside Your Favorite Half-Claimed Child, Dear Tallier of Payments Debts Work Days Weather Conditions Neighbors by Name and Race, Dear Borer of Wells,   Dear Master of Omission,

Were you a tear in her life, the kind
that starts with a moth hole and rips
to the seam overnight? She was sixteen
and newly freed, your cook and once
your slave. Was she peeling potatoes, shelling
peas, bent over an open flame in some back-
house kitchen when you came from behind
and prick!—your beard like brushfire
at her neck, how in battle exploding shells
set the wilderness and shrieking wounded alight.

Heard a whippoorwill holler this morning for the first time this spring. Heard a whippoorwill holler. All hands choking cotton. Heard a holler, a whimper. Heard a will whip her. Will heard a whip. Whip or will. Will heard. Herding hers. Whipping herds. Sowing oats. Whipping whores. Stripping cane or— whelped her willed her a well and a hold. Dank of the dark of the hell of the hold. Choking cotton. Caught in. A yoke and a pull. Stripped and caned for— Heard her holler, caught her, held her hand to the— whipped out your— held her head to the— whipped out the billfold. Heard a whimper this spring. Choked or— heard a holler, a hollowed-out hold, whipped to a wheelbarrow, hell-bent toward a hole, ripped from a wrapped in a gutwrench sugarhold.

Q: *So how did the women feel about this?*

A: *Don't guess they had no say.*

Peggy:

They carried us to Texas 'fore I knew
the horns of Sumter County from the tail
or how to tell directions from the way
moss creeps along a tree. If Mama thought
of running, she said nothing. She'd one day
have twenty children, every one a slave,
so she'd have been prime merchandise if they
had been inclined to sell, but luckily
they took her with the lot of us in big
ol' ox-drawn wagons, chained men following
on foot like livestock. Massa Bob then he
had thirty slaves the year we came, and by
the time he left for war, still more. Freedom
was more but less than a word, when he came down
home, banged up prisoner of war, flown. I
was cooking grits when he crept in on me,
tobacco stench. I was just sixteen in '66.

SCHEDULE 2.—Slave Inhabitants in _Beat No 9_ **in the County of** _Polk_ **State of** _Texas_ **, enumerated by me, on the** _19_ **day of** _July_ **, 1860.** _George Nelson_ **Ass't Marshal.**

283

SCHEDULE 2.—Slave Inhabitants in _Beat No 9_ **in the County of** _Polk_ **State of** _Texas_ **, enumerated by me, on the** _19_ **day of** _July_ **, 1860.** _George Nelson_ **Ass't Marshal.**

Courtesy of the National Archives and Records Administration

As a junior at Georgia Military Institute, Robert Wallace Hubert did not earn a single demerit. At nineteen he did not exhibit "mutinous conduct," disobey a superior, chat or sleep during study hours, miss a drill or roll call, or leave his coat unbuttoned in the ranks (no mention of his fly). Peggy would have been barely three, some unknown slave girl on his father's plantation, where the consequences of breaking the rules far outweighed an academic expulsion. I want to leave her there for a moment—before she was out of the sack-like shirt slave children wore, before she learned to cook. When I think of her later, I imagine burn scars rising up her arms, hair wrapped in coarse cloth to keep it out of the flames. *Someone's in the kitchen with Dinah*, her mother's name, her daughter's. Someone. Not some thing.

I used to teach critical inquiry to first-year composition students. You don't begin with a thesis, I told them, but through the process of seeking, discover the questions that have never occurred to you before. My father's cousin Bryant is eighty-two and does not hear well, so sometimes he answers a different question from the one I intended to ask. Last week Uncle Bryant told me what I already knew—that while still having children with his cook (and former slave) Peggy, my great-great-grandfather, Robert Wallace Hubert, had taken up with Peggy's sister Priscilla, too. I asked what the two women thought of this arrangement. "Don't guess they had no say."

Last night I read a *Smithsonian* article about PTSD in Civil War soldiers—then often mistaken for weakness, immorality, a failure of will. Recalling his experiences in a diary written fifty years after the war, Hubert never mentions the two years he spent in a Federal prison camp, nor much about the battles beyond a few facts and a brisk "I was in this campaign" before returning to his daily weather report, his rundown of the day's visitors and completed tasks.

I have lived in five regions and feel like an outsider everywhere, even in Los Angeles where I was raised. Here in Maui where I've landed days before my brother's wedding, I have just shed my family to stare at the beach. *I have heard the mermaids singing, each to each.* One autumn in New York I was so excruciatingly lonely that I could imagine loneliness driving a person to do something desperate. Loneliness a kind of agony. The last lines of a magazine poem Hubert copied into his diary: "What is home with none to meet,/ None to welcome, none to greet us./ Home is sweet, and only sweet,/ Where there's one who loves to meet us!" I want to tell him to get a cat, as I have. The purr and upturned belly. He had lost all or nearly all—wife, infant children, fortune (given that in 1860 his net worth consisted mostly of human beings), and, of course, the war. His loneliness crackled and burst into flame. What did it burn toward? And whom did it singe?

Now sunlight casts a shimmering vertical path across the waves. Beneath, I know from one hour on a submarine, there are sharks and eels and schools of beady-eyed fish who swim by, torqueing their bodies with enviable grace. There is a ship lurking on the bottom of the ocean, sunk intentionally to create a coral reef. Is this what we loners will become, a habitat for bottom feeders, when our minds come loose from their hinges and we are struggling to think?

Recently my therapist told me that trauma can alter a person's gene expression, so effectively we are all still paying for our ancestors' pain. I was skeptical. "But most of human history is trauma," I maintained. Later I repeated the theory to a retired psychologist at a dinner party. "That can't be," she said. "As a species we had to have been more resilient than that just to survive cave times."

Still I wonder at my solitary life—how I've blown myself to the four winds without a map or compass just to be a woman who owns her own person. Never have been anyone's girl. Is this what Peggy would have wished for? Could she even have imagined such an unchained way of being? The *Smithsonian* article warns against viewing 19th century Americans through "too contemporary a lens."

Another article in the same magazine suggests that time may not exist. Do moments build, or do they amass? "At issue is whether each subsequent moment is brought into existence from the previous moment by the passage of time. Think of a movie, back in the days when most movies were projected from actual reels of film. You could watch the movie, see what happened and talk sensibly about how long the whole thing lasted. But you could also sneak into the projection room, assemble the reels of film, and look at them all at once." I read this fifty minutes after toasting a new year, four hours before I would wake up with a hangover, two days before my brother and his fiancé will finally say "I do." Is Bob Hubert hovering here in the corridors of a resort on a Hawaiian island he might have read about in one of his newspapers, before or after its annexation? Is Peggy waiting in the wings, keys suspended from her apron strings? You can watch time unfold one scene after another, or you can take it all out at once and unfurl it across the beach. "The anti-time perspective says that the best way to think about the universe is ... as a collection of the frames."

When I get back to Wisconsin, I will start a Faulkner book club. We will meet a couple times a month and complain about the cold. *The past is never dead. It's not even past.* Here the ocean is bluer than the sky. In the distance a mountain dips into the bay.

—*Maui, January 1, 2015*

For two years after his wife Jenny's death, Bob would often
wake suddenly, her breath hot in his ear, her fine hair bent
against his eyelids and lips. He would wriggle into his army
coat with her taste on his tongue,

how salt and sweat mingled with lye lingering beyond the soap—on her neck,
her earlobes, the crook of her arm, even the corset laces she winced
against, the hoop skirt that made him think of a bell (ringing in his chest
in his groin in his gut), giddying at her touch, the lilt of her voice, her shy
kiss burning in him like rum, the night of the hop when suddenly
they were spinning, whizzing—and later that day in the belfry, just before
dark, taking her white gloved hand, he asked and asked again louder, his heart

pounding behind the boots of the Fifth New York Zouaves
and twice as fast, when the memory of Jenny overpowered
even the stinging stench of powder. He crammed a minié ball
into the Colt, aimed, and—

one of the Zouaves, shot
in the head, summersaulted
in midair, the tassels of his red
fez waving before it hit
the ground, just ahead of the man—
and Bob, in a daze, looked instinctively down, saw
the rent in his own gray pants, and—

After the battle, after they had chased the New Yorkers
through the branch, the Zouaves bogged down by their
soaking blouse pants, some pant legs so riddled with bullet
holes they spouted water with every step—he lay in a hospital
tent naked at the hip, and as the surgeon fumbled for the ball,
Bob reached for the press of Jenny's small palm but—

I have many a time been actually and painfully thirsty, and yet in sight of an ocean of fresh water.

—Decimus et Ultimus Barziza, Escaped POW

Sketch from the autograph book of Confederate Captain C. W. Fraser, courtesy of Johnson's Island Preservation Society

Johnson's Island/Winter 1863-64

That winter the pipes froze and no longer brought water in
from the bay. The guards ordered the men to dig two holes
about eight feet deep. They installed pumps, but still the water
is always exhausted within an hour of reveille. He has forgotten
to change his socks, and his toes are freezing in their own sweat.
The wind claws at his eyelids and lips, the ice is driving at him
in spikes—fearsome, and for a second he thinks the wind is
hammering nails into his face, that God Almighty is bent on
paling his grave. But no, he is grateful for the warmth of the
beard, ought to wrap it around him like a scarf (it is almost long
enough), his thirst gravel in his throat, his ears tingling and
then suddenly numb.

> *Heard a whippoorwill holler. Heard*
> *a holler, a whimper, a whirlpool,*
> *a snicker, heard a stag kick her.*

Long hours between roll call and roll call, he tries to rewrite
his own history, to erase the moment his ears popped charging
a Pennsylvania hill—

Whip 'em, boys. Whipped or— not whipped
yet. (How you begin to doubt your own head—

a shell exploding ahead and even the screams of the man beside
    you are muted, like cries from the shore when you are holding your breath
underwater—the line's a scattered mess of boulders, but you're yelling *Stand firm* (why?),
    the rebel yell issuing from your own spent breath though you cannot hear but
for a moment think you will make it to the top despite gunfire hailing
    down, the forest a dizzying maze of smoke and half-blinded, retching, you run
headlong into a tree before you are taken (how?)—sword in the back, see yourself
    relinquishing your revolver to a first lieutenant from New York, some retribution
        for Second Manassas, the blue columns at Fredericksburg melting away—)

Look away, look away. The boy who disarmed him was younger than he, had curious auburn eyes that reminded Bob of some dogs he'd seen.

H | 5 | Tex.

R. W. Hubert
Capt. Co K, 5 Regt Texas

Appears on a register of

Prisoners of War

at Fort Delaware, Del.

Where captured Gettysburg, Pa.

When captured July 2 , 1863.

When joined post July 7 , 1863.

Remarks: Forwarded to Johnson's Island in charge Lt Geo. W. Ahl, July 18. 1863.

Fort Delaware, Del., Register No. 4; page 32

(639)   J B Dowd
                                         Copyist.

HEAD-QUARTERS DISTRICT OF TEXAS
GALVESTON, TEXAS, JUNE 19, 1865*

The people of Texas are informed that, in accordance with a Proclamation from the Executive of the United States, all Peggies are free. This involves absolute equality of rights, and rights of property between former Roberts and Peggies, and the connection heretofore existing between them becomes that of redbeard and free whippoorwill.

The black bottoms are advised to remain at their present homes and work for wages. They are informed that they will not be allowed to collect at Military Posts, and that they will not be supported in idleness, there or elsewhere.

2nd: As a result of said liberation, persons formerly Peggies are guaranteed the right to make songs disposing of their services to their former Roberts or other parties, but with the distinct understanding that they are blue bandannas and shall be held responsible for the performance of their part of the song to the same extent that the redbeard is bound to pay for the consideration for the whippoorwilling performed.

3rd: Unless other regulations are promulgated by the Black Bottoms' Bureau, the amount and kind of consideration for whippoorwilling shall be a matter of song between redbeard and blue bandanna.

4th: All colored persons are earnestly enjoined to remain with their former Roberts until permanent arrangements can be made and thus secure the crop of the present season and at the same time promote the interests of themselves, their redbeard and the Commonwealth.

Sister Pris in plush petals and sass. Hissing
a whisper, plenty's a pistol. Purse plundered
pull of the piney woods. Just a flash
of the drawers, a whiff of the door. Plucked
a bow, plumped a foal, heard a whippoorwill
holler and down bird, blow.

need air need light need breath caught in the gap if not gasping
she says I am not   I was not—
hold it she says   in the tree's blasted ear   not she says—
knot he pulls   naught he hears
she says not here   hollow hollering into the tree its ear

in the bark an incision   a rib   a spare   brook does not
babble
that's laughter   it peals

In the 1880 census, Robert Wallace Hubert is living with Peggy, whose full name was Margaret. She is listed as his servant, and their six "mulatto" children are identified as his. Peggy is only thirty, younger than I am as I sit writing this. She had started bearing children by eighteen. By 1880 Peggy could read and write, but her sister Priscilla, listed separately as a head of household not far away, could only read.

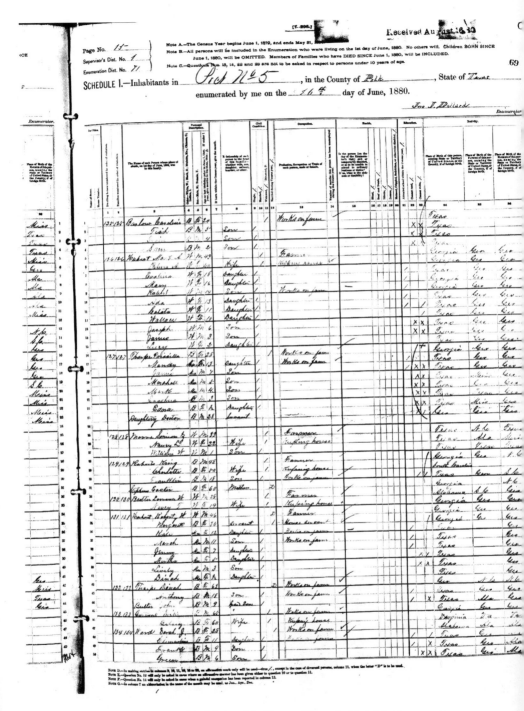

In 1883, the State Convention of Colored Men of Texas protested a miscegenation law that punished interracial marriage but not interracial sex. Its purpose was clear. "A careful consideration of the operation of the law convinces all fair-minded persons, that the law was intended to gratify the basest passions of certain classes of men who do not seek such gratification by means of lawful wedlock." The Convention recommended an amendment to the law "that will punish as rigidly for all carnal intercourse between the two races, unlawfully carried on, as it punishes them for intermarrying." Of course no such amendment ever came into being.

nounce that the law bears its evil fruits. The committee dismiss the consideration of this dark subject with the recommendation that the Convention urge upon our next Legislature the necessity of an amendment to this law that will punish as rigidly for all carnal intercourse between the two races, unlawfully carried on, as it punishes them for intermarrying. If the Legislature do this, they will show a willingness to stop the tide of immorality that now makes such inroads upon the morals of some of our most promising females.

Double standards between men and women's sexual behavior were not lost on Bob Hubert. In 1892 he copied two poems on the subject from magazines he'd read. One is called "The Prodigal Daughter," the other "Two Sinners." "And boys will be boys, the old folks say./ And the man's the better who's had his way." In a bed? On the floor? In a cornfield? Or an orchard? In the henhouse? Or the woods?

In *The Black Family in Slavery and Freedom*, Herbert G. Gutman writes, "Ex-slave women everywhere dealt with a legacy that viewed them as dependent sexual objects."

Two Sinners.

There was a man, it was said one time,
Who went astray in his youthful prime.
Can the brain keep cool & the heart keep quiet
When the blood is a river that is running riot?
And boys will be boys, the old folks say,
And the man's the better who's had his way.

The sinner reformed, & the preacher told
Of the prodigal son who came back to the fold.
And christian people threw open the door
With a warmer welcome than ever before.
Wealth & honor were his to command,
And a spotless woman gave him her hand.
And the world strewed their pathway with flowers
      a-bloom.
      "God bless Lady & God bless groom."

There was a maiden went astray
In the golden dawn of her life's young day.
She had more passion's heart than head,
And she followed blindly where fond love led,
And love unchecked is a dangerous guide
To wander at will by a fair girls' side.

The woman repented & turned from sin,
But no door opened to let her in:
The preacher prayed that she might be forgiven,
But told her to look for mercy in heaven.
For this is the law of the earth we know
That the woman is scorned, while the man may go
A brave man wedded her after all,
But the world said frowning, "We shall not call
                    Ella Wheeler Wilcox

I meet a distant relative on an online genealogy site who has been researching the Huberts for years. She shares a story I have never heard. I call it the myth of the slave savior. In this story, Bob Hubert is in a prison camp when he asks one of his female slaves to come help him in a time of great need. The distant relative who tells me this story has heard it from a descendant of Priscilla but concludes that Priscilla was too young at the time, and either her mother, Dinah, or sister Peggy must have been the "slave angel." (I imagine this character as a Disney heroine, the slave savior with a long neck and twig of a waist, decked out in perfectly tailored scraps with her faithful sidekick, perhaps a whippoorwill, riding stoically on her head.)

Needless to say I am skeptical. I have never heard this story, and why would an enslaved woman travel thousands of miles to Union lines without taking her freedom? An expert at Johnson's Island Preservation Society reports,

> *I have heard that five of the prisoners captured from Port Hudson, La. brought servants with them to Johnson's Island. I have not heard that any of the Gettysburg prisoners bringing slaves or servants. Under normal conditions no prisoner could receive visitors unless severely ill and then only with the doctor's OK. I find it highly unlikely that a slave (or former slave) would be allowed to visit.*

My relative is not convinced—says it could have been one of the other prison camps in Delaware and Maryland that Hubert passed through briefly, staying for a few days or a week at a time, that he could have sent word ahead of his arrival. I wonder why she is so intent on believing this.

In the myth of the slave savior, she (Peggy, Priscilla, Dinah) is an actor rather than acted upon. I picture her arriving at night, exhausted from the journey, covered in muck. She knows what she is doing when she pulls off the kerchief, lets down her hair. And when she puts it up again.

Or she doesn't know. When is the last time any of these men has seen a woman, white or colored, any woman at all? She is trembling as she wades among these armies of men, feels the thin fabric of the dress sticking to her thighs, her breasts. She is as sweaty as the prisoners who call out lewd suggestions, egged on by the guards. Both Rebs and Yankees tug on her skirt, her tattered shawl. When a general reaches for her, her skin goes clammy. She has swallowed her voice like a seed.

We want to believe that she is a heroine here, that she has some agency, that for once in her life she was given a choice.

Peggy:

The night before my water broke I dreamt
I bore a chimney babe into the world.
The cord it swung from her brick neck and ash
was streaming down her leg. Flames swaggered, reared,
charred her skin, hot poker hands unwound
her shift. I woke ablaze, my petticoat
drenched, roped his stiff beard round my neck,
and "She won't work in no white man's damn kitchen,"
I said. That beard reeked gunpowder, whiskey, Pris.

*

The winter she learned about Priscilla, she kept her lips
pursed, her hands always busy with the corn or collards
or wrapped in one of the children's hair. But at night he
would wake in a sudden stab of pain, her knee jabbing into
his old war wound in what she pretended were the throes
of a nightmare, and he who had been the master would
allow this transgression—a brief reproach before he jerked
the knee away carelessly, like an errant boll of cotton fallen
into his path.

Peggy rises out of sleep through the dream called Blue—where all her kinfolks are wading through fields of blue, even her father left in Georgia, her stillborn brother somehow grown, her niece who stumbled into the fire on Christmas day and died with the vision of her white dress aflame, the aunt or uncle who ran off or was lost forever to the auction block. They are all wearing blue—blue hats, blue shawls, and in the way they sing a song with no words, deep from the gut, there is also blue, and bluely she creeps toward them in her calico blue, and now there is a dance, they are partnering for the quadrille, and the man they called Bo Peep cradles a banjo, strikes a tune, blue, and her petticoat's starched with hominy water, and Pris's, too, and every time they stop moving for a second the petticoats pop, and Pris giggles, and in Pris's eyes are flecks of blue. The log train shakes her into waking, black then dark blue, and she reaches for her kerchief blue, and she is stumbling toward the cradle blue and cooing *Shoo shoo* to the baby who is hollering now. One Sunday the preacher prayed, "Lord, let us all go to Heaven where there'll be no log train." *Who who who* and a clankety clank—*whose?* Black smoke curling into the half blue.

In the summer of 2013, I acquired a copy of Bob Hubert's diaries—one diary he kept from 1889 to 1894 and one five-month fragment of a diary from 1917, ending just three months before his death. The diaries took me a year to type. Squinting over 225 pages of Bob's crisp handwriting, I began to feel a strange intimacy with this great-great-grandfather, as though I were tugging on some line tossed across a hundred and twenty years, and he was holding onto the other end.

In Bob Hubert's diaries, the silences speak louder than what's said—so I developed a practice of reading for absence. When I saw the names of Bob's mixed-race children (very frequently) or their mothers (less frequently), it was less like a lightbulb switching on in my head than a fog lifting momentarily only to reform again. Though I might carve my own small portholes out of the haze, I would never get a clear view. Because, although Bob reports his children's comings and goings, bores a well for Peggy, hoes her cotton and sets out her potato vines, and spends hours in the field alongside their son Plunk, clearly the apple of his eye, he never explains why. Bob may occasionally point out, extraneously, that Plunk or Bill Hubert is "colored," but in the diary Bob never says who these *colored* people are to him, though his white relatives are usually identified by family relationship—"bro.," "nephew," "niece," "grand niece."

Who is Bob's intended reader? Who is he considering when he writes, "In opening my book I see that I skipped these two pages and therefore if any one ever reads this book they must skip to page 160 and then turn back." To move forward in this narrative, you must palm through the past.

"A slave and a white man fell into a well.
Who do you think the master rescued?"
Bob asks Plunk on the way to Chester.
"It wasn't my place, mind," he adds, cradling
a curl on the boy's head. "This was back
in Georgia, long before the war." Plunk shivers,
running through times tables, whole ledgers
of dollar signs he cannot multiply. "Sir,"
he says, clutching the wool he'll sell from sheep
he's shorn himself. What happened to the white
man, deep in the well, once they hauled the slave
out? Did he poison the water for years,
free and slave alike strangely ill, drinking
his unsalable decomposing flesh?

faired off a thin shade
Bob's bogged down in the gin way
fault pulling fodder

right smart ache o'clock
pin raceknife half-chain survey
Peg stain or Pris shade

making a bed tick
found her complaining and went
kin split a shade singe

whippoorwill freight ague
a norther sang coughing cane
split member engine

cane stripped all hands bent
carried to brought from went down
July ground gin town

into the branch she
fair went down a shade too tan
Bob's song a noon drown

cat eye salt her spine
cork tight branch bottom July
shame upon me I—

In *A Pictorial History of Polk County*, published in 1976, there are hundreds of pictures of Polk County residents from the mid-19th century through the early 20th. There are photographs of log rollings and butchered hogs, of baptisms and baseball teams—one white and one Alabama and Coushatta, from "Indian Village." Assuming that blackness is a visible trait (while knowing that it isn't), there is only one picture of a black person, identified as "Uncle Duck," a "faithful slave brought by the Darby family from Alabama to Texas." He reportedly chose not to leave them when freedom came. In two other photographs black men appear along with whites, but captions identify only the white people, as though the identities of the black men have been erased. No black women are pictured anywhere at all.

Peggy/ An Inventory

She has a recipe for cornbread and one for curing hog cholera and another for keeping quiet and another for children born too close together. She has a cast iron skillet and a pale blue bandanna and a steel thimble she slips over her finger when she works up a quilt, a shirt, a song. She has a wash pot and a boiling stick and a fear of ha'nts and a way of looking twice over her shoulder. She has an apron she rips into rags in one smooth motion and a song for every kind of weather but days when the sun will not shine out. She has a butcher knife and a paring knife, a knife for extracting chiggers, a knife for scraping hogs, and a knife she hides under her bed before births to soften the pain. She has a deep belly groan like the HE&WT Railway grinding toward Houston, and even her lullabies crack like kindling. No one will own to hearing her cry, but her laugh is the crash of breaking glass—sharp, high, and exactingly brief.

Bob:

Can I be your lazy eye, your wander-
lust, your grave without a headstone,
your bleeding gums, your buck teeth
and your walk bowlegged at the knee? Can
I be your fortune hunter, your glimpse
of wild geese, your red russet shoes
that poison the feet? Reckon this is the best
of my seed. Been stripping cane and blind
robbing the bees. Reckon you've thought
of swimming the creek. Last night they came
on horseback, white hoods like phantoms
scanning the trees, burning torches, shattering
sleep. I dragged the shotgun from the door
and stepped squinting onto the porch.

Not all sexual ties between slave women and white men were exploitative, and not all interracial contacts between slaves, ex-slaves and free persons involved black women and white men.

—Herbert G. Gutman, *The Black Family in Slavery and Freedom, 1750-1925*

Boring a well down
Peggy's house, Jeff Stewart and
Mark & March helping me — Peggy
She has been on a visit to her Kin
in Houston — Peggy got home last night
Hoeing cotton & set
out potato vines this evening
at Peggy's house

She watches him ride out at dawn, tossed onto the
saddle like a sack of gunpowder left in the rain.
"God forgive me I am drunk," he said, he slurred,
he sang, last night, staggering into the washstand,
toppling the pitcher, shattering the vase, scattering
her black-eyed susans, her bluebonnets, her
patience and her easy shame. He didn't even
bother to sidestep the puddle, hands already
taking the bearings of her breasts. She almost said,
"Hush," but instead, "I was putting the children
to bed," like a slap. Now he is singing "The
Yellow Rose of Texas," all mucked up by
Confederates: *She's the sweetest rose of color this soldier
ever knew*—and she steps into black land gumbo
clay on her way to the creek. "You forgot your
damn compass," she thinks, sinking deep, deep.

Night sky arcs, an upturned bowl
splattered with stars. This week
if all goes as planned, I'll be an aunt.

Jan 8 Wednesday 1890 (Bob Hubert's diary)—

Peggy got home last night. She has been on a visit to her kin in
Houston ever since the 23rd Dec. Planting oats to day.

I will tell my nephew what I cannot know:

When Peggy left, Jim Crow
comb stayed home. Bucked
the brass tooth, hair raged loose.

She came back singing "We Born
To Die" night after night. I will tell my nephew
I do not know the tune, but I will sing it for you.

The bowl was rocking overhead.
She could not cry, head
filled with water, her face a bog. Not
that it's a sorrow song—some hymn, prayer

to a god she must have believed in though I do not.
We born to die, she sang, shuck mop aloft,
raising red dust. "All of us," she said, "but One."

I do not know the tune, but I will hum
it for you. Jim Crow comb stayed home, sky
that Christmas an upturned bowl.

She did not know, for instance, that if a board comes loose from the rafters, a barn cat will catch a bird by the throat and haul it in through the gap. (When you walk in, you must holler and stamp until the cat drops its prey and the swallow flies out.) She did not know what happened to her father back in Georgia or how to dance the polka or the names of any of her ancestors' gods. She did not know the Latin words for "slave" or "freedom," "work" or "fever," but she did know the word for love and heard her daughters repeating it when they thought no one was listening. "Amor," they'd whisper, Laly to Jennie, Jennie to Tid, all wrapped in a quilt, some early morning, giggling. Peggy would give a gentle "tut tut," remind them of the eggs to fetch, and go on dusting, because she had never been young and puddin' headed like that.

Louisa, listed as Louisa Perryman on her son Bill's death certificate, was an older sister of Peggy and Priscilla, another of their mother Dinah's twenty children. I know little about the men who fathered these children, whether there were two or three or more, whether they disappeared by force or by choice, whether they were sold away or killed among the "Negro labor" sent to the Confederates to fortify Galveston. Whether black or white or whether one, Lucius Thorpe, might account for the appearance of Priscilla's children, said to look "part Indian." *Until death or distance do you part*, the marriage vows for enslaved people read. Not read—*said*.

These men, whom Dinah may have loved or hated or tolerated, left their surnames on her children, but there's only so far I can trace my own progenitor, father of Peggy Guerry Hubert and several of her siblings. When Peggy was born around 1849 or '50, the Huberts, along with the people they enslaved, were living in Sumter County, Georgia, in the neighborhood of a James P. Guerry, owner of thirty-three human beings. Thus I imagine that Peggy's father was either a Guerry or Guerry property and that the Huberts' move to Texas separated him from his family. Perhaps he was already gone, since Priscilla, only two or three years younger than Peggy, carries a different surname. Priscilla's father, Lucius Thorpe or Tharpe, was probably a slave of the Huberts or Turners, transported from Georgia to Texas with the rest of the chattel. He remained with Dinah in Polk County after the Civil War, while Louisa lived in the next household with her three children, two fathered by a black man or men and one by Bob Hubert. When I discover an 1874 marriage record for a Louisa Perryman and "Lucias Tharpe," I don't know what to make of it. Did Louisa marry her stepfather? Between the 1870 and 1880 censuses, Dinah and Lucius divorced, Lucius either died or left the vicinity, and Louisa changed her name to Tillman and bore three more children, all classified as black and not mulatto like Bill.

Priscilla is "Pris Thorpe" in the diaries Bob Hubert kept between 1889 and 1894, and Peggy appears thrice as "Peggy" and once as "Margaret Hubert," who, Bob takes care to explain, "used to be my cook." Bob's diary never mentions Louisa at all, probably because she was already long gone, though she had borne him at least one son, Bill, probably in 1868. Bill lived a long life as a Polk County carpenter, a trade he shared with his half-brothers Mark and Plunk. But Louisa disappeared, into marriage and widowhood and then a second or third marriage, a name change, before vanishing for good into an unknown grave. Because she seems to have successfully exited the scene or at least the archive, I think of Louisa as the one who got away. But got away to where—and what?

Of the three sisters or half-sisters who bore Bob Hubert's children, Peggy, "who used to be my cook," is the one he kept closest, whose sons he left land and whose daughters he educated. Was Peggy, perhaps the most confined of the three, also, within the constrictions of her time, the most secure? It seems that at least her children were. Did Bob provide for them because there was no question of paternity, because Peggy, who bore children to no other man, was his and his alone?

But what about Louisa, the one who got away, who was banished or escaped: What was her favorite color? If I looked her in the eye, would her gaze meet mine or dart off center? Did she ever toss her headwrap into the fire and dress her hair in violets? Did she sing off key or hit the notes home like her nephew Jesse Hubbard batting left handed? Did she ever see him play, or was she long gone by then? Was pleasure even a woman's game to dabble in?

Peggy is trimming her sentences into strips, heed shorn of the wind to gut forth. If she won't thrust into the meat to speak, it is seldom because she has nothing to say. Pris spins blue yarns, hangs her pots in cranes swung high over the flames. Pris is tall, Peggy low. If there are words between them (and nobody knows), it is Peggy who will rake them slow. Could say, "You tore your drawers with me," but no. Gutting a cabbage to wrap corn pones, Pris hands her a knife a shade too dull—   sings *Peggy does you love me now?*

Once when Pris was twelve her mother
saw her crossing the field near dusk with
her dress riding up. Dinah called her
over, stooped, and pulled out the hem in
front of everyone and Peggy, who was
about to laugh but caught their mother's
eye, grunted "Uh uh," instead.

[Show a Witness:]

I am rereading Dawn Lundy Martin's book *Life in a Box
Is a Pretty Life*, which asks the question: When there is no
choice, when the box is inescapable, then what?

My alarm goes off at midnight. I don't remember setting it.
I carry the book to the bedroom. I am going to look up the
word "phantasmagoric." My phone has finished charging,
and before accessing my Merriam-Webster app, I check
Facebook and find that an unarmed nineteen-year-old
black man has been killed by a Madison police officer near
Williamson and Few. There is, or has been, a "gathering" at
the site. That would be a half-hour walk for me at midnight
in the cold. I am not going. But I remember how the cop
car slowed as I was rounding my corner this afternoon,
how I noticed the grill on the backseat window, stared at
the bars. Of course, there are many cops in Madison. And I
live across the street from their parking garage.

What about when there is no choice, when the box is ines-
capable, then what?

In Madison, where there are hardly any black people, in
Dane County where black adults between eighteen and
fifty-four make up 4.9% of the population that age but
52.4% of the incarcerated population, I live half a block from
the county jail, which is euphemistically named the Public
Safety Building. There I see more black people coming and
going than I ever see on my walk to work, on my walk to the
grocery store to the bank to the pet store to the coffee shop,
or certainly in my classroom at the University of Wisconsin,
where I have had only one black student this year. And so

when I walk home I wonder if passersby think I am getting out of jail. Or visiting someone. Or posting bail.

On a comment thread in response to an article about a Black Lives Matter rally last fall, someone said something like, "Black people are 5% of the population of Dane County and 50% of that 5% are criminals."

It turns out that Tony Robinson, "the unarmed black man" killed by a Madison police officer, had a white mother. I also have a white mother.

In Madison, I have become black.

In L.A. and New York, I never identified as black. Even in Pittsburgh where there is no middle ground, I would say, "My dad is black." I was partly distancing myself from an "undesirable" degree of blackness—the "internalized racism" I could recognize but not quite expunge—and I was partly resisting the urge to make a claim I could not deliver on. For me, the right to blackness always felt unearned. (Aren't I a white girl on the phone?)

In Madison, I have become black.
Is this inextricably linked to my hatred of Madison?

phantasmagoria: 1: an exhibition of optical effects and illusions. 2a : a constantly shifting complex succession of things seen or imagined. b: a scene that constantly changes. 3: a bizarre or fantastic combination, collection, or assemblage

From the diary of Robert Wallace Hubert, February 1, 1890, a Saturday:

This evening just at night went over to the Blair creek school house to a sleight of hand show. And witnessed a little girl walk a tight wire & some very good sleight of hand tricks.

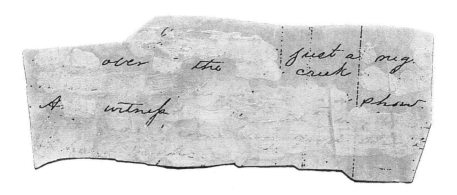

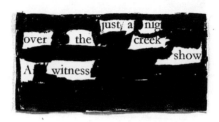

over   the   just a nig
                    creek
                            show
A   witness

The magician's hand has slipped. Or is he a trick?

What about when there is no choice, when the box is
inescapable, then what?

—*Madison, March 7, 2015*

In my high school U.S. history class, when we got to the part on the inhumanity of slave holders, I said, "Actually, I am descended from slave holders." For some reason nobody stated the obvious: that I am also descended from slaves.

Some calls them "Bright" niggers, but I calls them "No Nation,"
'cause that what they is.

—Adeline Marshall, ex-slave, Texas narratives

Jesse Hubbard was Bob's youngest child and Priscilla's youngest as well, born in 1895. He was educated only through the fifth grade. In 1972, Jesse told a researcher he had been working in a sawmill when he started playing baseball professionally in 1911.

What Jesse didn't say: In April of 1911, "Jess Hubert" pleaded guilty to "unlawfully gaming" and was committed to the Polk County Jail until a $10 fine and an unspecified "cost" were paid. The costs must have been more than the fine, because Jesse's older brother Mark paid $15 in June and the remaining $5.50 near the end of August—four months, presumably, that Jesse sat in jail while Mark was scraping together the money. Mark held onto the court receipts, which are still in the family. "Those Huberts didn't take no mess off of nobody," Mark's grandson James Robert Hubert tells me. He says that's when Jesse decided to go to California. He did move there eventually, in 1935 near the end of his baseball career, but in 1911 the teenager's escape was more immediate.

This is the version Jesse told the researcher, or at least this is the version the researcher decided to print: "In 1911, when I was 16, a guy gave me $25 a week, room and board, to play ball. Then I got $50 a week. Went to Beaumont and got $100 a week. We had a league— Houston, Beaumont, Dallas, Austin. I lost only three games. I was a tough man in my day."

The State of Texas,
vs
Jess Hubert

1176

April 24th - 1911.

On this day this cause came on to
be heard, Hon. P.R. Rowe, regular judge presiding
State appeared by her co atty Geo Bean. Deft
appeared in person, Each announced ready for
trial. Whereupon Deft waived his right of trial by a
jury & pleaded guilty to information filed herein
charging said Deft with offense of unlawfully
gaming. The Court having heard & duly considered
same. It is ordered, adjudged & decreed by
the Court that said Deft be & he is now here
adjudged guilty as charged & his punishment
is assessed at a fine of $10.00
Wherefore it is considered by the Court
that the State of Texas, do have & recover of &
from said Deft said sum of $10.00 & that
all his cost be paid, he be committed to
co jail until all said fine & cost be paid.

Courtesy of the Sam Houston Regional Library and Research Center

Jesse "Mountain" Hubbard:

Man, I beat those guys so bad it was pitiful!
The team that wanted me was the Tigers.
They didn't sign me because Ty Cobb was there,
and he didn't like colored no kind of way.

The team that wanted me bad was the Tigers.
If Cobb saw us coming, he sat out the game.
He didn't like colored no kind of way.
He'd grip the ball tight and bug his eyes.

If Cobb saw us coming, he sat out the game.
They used to accuse me of cheating, of cutting
the ball. He'd grip the ball tight and bug
his eyes. Well, I had something I could cut it with.

They used to accuse me of cheating, of cutting the ball.
If they threw drop balls in front of the plate, I'd kill
them. Well I had something I could cut it with.
All I did was pull up my pants like this.

If they threw drop balls in front of the plate,
I'd kill them. Now that's part of the history of the Negro
race. All I did was pull up my pants like this.
When I got warmed up real good, I cut loose on them.

Now that's part of the history of the Negro race.
They didn't sign me because Ty Cobb was there.
When I got warmed up real good, I cut loose
on them. Man, I beat those guys so bad it was pitiful!

*This big, light-complexioned Texan, who was nicknamed
"Mountain," was part Indian and almost passed for white to
make it to the major leagues, but destiny dictated that his career
would be spent entirely in the Negro Leagues. The New York
Giants sent him to their farm team in Massena, New York,
and tried to pass him as white, and the Detroit Tigers were
among several teams that expressed an interest, but none took
the risk to sign him.*

—Negro Leagues Baseball Museum

He acts like the cock of the walk or the ham
of the land, spoke of the folk, peg of the keg,
suds of the mud. He rides in on his luck,
double chuck batter up, pitched from an itch,
mountain man hits, mountain swagger and lip,
mudslide's sway and tip.

JESSE HUBBARD
IN HERO ACT

LOS ANGELES—(ANP)— Somewhere in the wide confines of Los Angeles there are 3 white hoodlums nursing cuts and bruises handed out to them by a lone defender of Negro women, but nevertheless they are perhaps gloating over the fact they got "even" by smashing a $50 plate glass window in one of the finest hotels in the city. The principals in the exciting episode were the unknown white trio, Jesse Hubbard, former Negro National league ball player, a colored Black and White Taxicab Co. starter, and two dining car waiters. The hotel in question is the Clark hotel.

Hubbard, who is six feet in height and very powerful was standing on the sidewalk in front of the hotel about one o'clock last Wednesday morning. A car bearing the three whites drew up to the club opposite them and one stepped out on the running board. Accosting the colored men who were quietly conversing prior to retiring, he said, "Say, we're looking for some girls, where can we find them?" Hubbard answered: "Go down to the Biltmore hotel, you'll find plenty." "Oh, no, we mean colored girls," another of the three rejoined.

Too surprised at their effrontery to act, the others only stared, but Hubbard quickly stepped down off the curb and faced them.

"Just a minute, I'll help you," he said, meanwhile loosing a terrific right that landed on the jaw of the one on the running board knocking him off. Then whirling around the side of the car, the driver still at the wheel, he hit him a terrific blow square on the mouth, splitting his lip wide open. As he turned his attention to the other occupant of the sedan, his victim began begging off, but to no avail.

"Don't hit me, don't hit me," pleaded "I didn't say anything."

But Hubbard's anger was up, and as the fellow attempted to run, he gave him a kick that sent him sprawling on his face. As Hubbard ceased his hostilities, the defeated trio piled into their car and drove away. Thinking the incident ended, the colored men again grouped in front of the hotel, but in a few moments the car with the three men in it returned, having merely circled the block.

One was standing on the running board, and as the car slowed down, he hurled a big empty bottle at the group. All ducked just in time and the missile crashed thru the big plate glass window that fronts the hotel lobby. They then sped away and disappeared. As their lights were out, none of the colored men was able to discern the car's number so police have been unable to locate the culprits.

A hero act Hubbard hurled.
In black and white. Three white
men drew up. "Say, we're looking
for some girls. Oh no, we mean
colored girls." In black and white,
that hurler loosed a terrific
right. White hoodlums nursing
their surprise, pled "Don't hit
me don't hit me." They circled
wide and smashed a window
in black and white.

~~NO-RUN NO-HIT GAME~~
Hubbard Pitches Perfect ~~Ball,~~
Toy~~ing With Logan Square~~

~~ATLANTIC CITY, N.J. JULY 6~~
~~(Special). Bacharach Giants made~~
~~it a clean sweep of the series by~~
~~blanking Logan Square, 12 to 0.~~
~~Hubbard did~~ **not allow** ~~a hit or~~
~~run and not a visitor reach~~**ed**
~~second, four reaching first on free~~
passes. ~~Ad Swidler was hit to all~~
~~corners for twenty-three bases,~~
~~including two home runs.~~

Hubbard in Form.

PATER/SON, ~~N.J., Aug. 8~~
~~Jess~~ **Hubbard,** ~~the "Texas~~
hurling ~~wizard," was~~ **in fine**
~~fettle today and let the heavy-~~
~~hitting~~ **Silk Sox** ~~down with no~~
~~hits. "Ace" Clinton who recently~~
~~tamed the fast-going Hilldale~~
~~boys,~~ **was "easy meat" for the**
~~Brooklynites and they climbed~~
~~on him for nine solid sm~~**ashes**
~~combined with two errors,~~
~~resulting in six runs. 6,000 fans~~
~~saw the game. Score, 6 to 0.~~

Courtesy of the late Bryant Hubert

The pain that opens the door is brisk and gut eyed. It staggers in its brogans, dragging its death, a tin pail stocked from the rubbish sack. When it sprawls upon you smelling of the Big Thicket, scratching your neck with its homespun and switches, you barely wince. Now the pain is inhaling you in drags, and you hear the shuck mop clattering, the paddle for gathering butter from the churn. The pain peels back your brow, its blue hymn bleeding indigo as it dips out of tune.

I want to think that when the witness
tree leaned into the ledge, it heard her heart
stop between one breath and the next.

The day they buried Peggy, all the trees
were whispering, the chinkapins and loblolly
pines. Did she miscarry, bleed to death
while Bob or Plunk saddled the horse, rode
miles panting after the doctor in town? Did she recall
her mother's twenty pregnancies and bite her lips
her tongue   the quilt   and finally the bedpost lest
her daughters hear her scream and come too close? Did she rage
deliriously through the shakes? Bloat from dropsy or hack
through a consumptive fit? Or did she take her own life—
swallow strychnine or arsenic, hang herself from a beam, clench
a shotgun between her teeth?

Peggy sometimes spoke in whispers. Sometimes
she did not speak at all but just said "Uh *huh*,"
leaning hard on the last syllable, or "*Sho'* did,"
with all her weight on the first. Sometimes
if Bob looked closely, he would see a thought blow
across her face. Once he might have tried to squeeze
it out, but a woman is not sugar cane you can run
through a mill, its secrets easily expelled.

Peggy:

Today I plucked a whippoorwill from down
the bottom of the well. Her neck was broke
but still she hollered out her name. "Get.
The burst of freedom came in June. Go yon-
                              der way," I said.

Once when she was sixteen, Peggy finished cooking the
hominy and drew pictures with ashes left on the hearth.

I am not a cook or a Captain. I have never
been a slave or a slaveholder, a soldier or a
chattel. I was not born in Georgia and carried
to Texas. I was not raised in a slave cabin or
trained at a military academy. I was never
counted as an asset or a casualty of battle. I
have never been considered three fifths of a
person or anybody's master. I have not paled a
grave or ploughed a field. All my fields are
figurative, and if I say they are furrowed, I am
only referring to a momentary fold between
my brows. Most of my feelings are caught in
my throat. Or deadweight in the bottom of a
well, bloating with the white man's corpse.
How the heft of history is sinking me still—
and I don't even fight it, don't even kick.

I flew to Texas twelve days after a breakup. It had been a short relationship but my only romance in years. The breakup coincided with the end of the semester and the end of my fellowship in Madison—what should have been a moment of possibility but instead felt like too many doors resoundingly slamming shut.

My lover left me because I was impossible to read. "I think I would have fallen in love with you," she said, "if I could see my emotions reflected on your face." But I am as inscrutable as chalk. The lover who left me is white. She studies epigenetics, which suggests that external factors can affect gene expression. The question of ancestral trauma looms large. I wanted to reach for those scars (cards)—but did not. How many centuries on the auction block?

When I was a child, three or four years old, often when I cried my father would threaten me, "If you don't stop crying, I'll give you something to cry about!" He was raised by parents who might now be classed as refugees from the South, two of the 140,000 African Americans who migrated to Los Angeles in the 1940s. During the Second World War, my grandfather claimed, he could make as much from three months of work in an L.A. shipyard as he could in a year as a black schoolteacher in segregated Waco, where he'd been paid half the salary of his white counterpart. My father was the oldest child, the unexpected gift who arrived thirteen years into his parents' marriage. They loved him absolutely. And his mother made him *choose* a switch from the peach tree when she thought he needed serious disciplining. The worst I ever got was a spanking.

A few days after my arrival in Texas, my parents flew from L.A. to Houston, where I met them, and the three of us drove to Polk County in a thunderstorm, the rain beating against the car, lightning snapping overhead. We met cousins we had never heard of before, cousins who had not known we existed. Cousin Ralph showed us the house that belonged to my father's Granny Dinah, the sixth child of Bob and Peggy. My father remembered Dinah's ghost stories told in that home in Seven Oaks—a squat clapboard house off the highway with a pitch roof and plank steps teetering up to a raised porch, a house that belongs to lush woods and heat waves rising like steam. I stepped onto the septic tank to take a photograph and walked right into the poison oak.

When he saw my great-grandmother Dinah's grave, Daddy said, "My first memory is of Granny Dinah." In retrospect, he knows it was the day of his little sister's funeral. "The funeral home was right down the block, and Granny Dinah was walking me home." The little sister who died at birth was the second of my grandparents' three children, named Geneva after her mother. The hospital where she was born, where she died, was one of only two hospitals in Los Angeles that my grandparents knew to accept black patients in 1949. They were sure the whites-only hospitals had better equipment.

I was born with a misplaced artery over three decades later in the same county. Armed with private health insurance, I was seven months old when I went into surgery, and all that remains from the experience is a scar that arches from the base of my left breast to the curve of my shoulder blade. By the early '80s, we had bought our way into what were once whites-only hospitals. There were times when the matter of race could cede to the matter of class—or the lines of exclusion were redrawn so who was in and who was out had shifted ever so slightly with the times. And unlike my infant aunt, I would survive, fallen, this time, on the safer side of the line.

My Grandpa Russell had a thing about Africa and made snide remarks—about the cousin who gave his children "nonsense" Swahili names and "those Africans" at church who only put a dollar in the collection plate. When I was ten or twelve Grandpa said something like, "What's this 'back to Africa'? You want to swing from trees?" Grandpa had blue-black eyes. I do not want to say the closest color was sapphire. I do not want to say my grandpa was a dark-skinned black man with eyes like sapphires. I want to say my grandpa's eyes lied, but that's not right. Their view of the truth was large. Grandpa was a five-year-old in Waco when a white mob fifteen thousand strong burned Jesse Washington alive. Once Grandpa said, "I haven't seen lynchings, but I've seen the results of lynchings." My grandpa of the blue-black eyes did not lie, but his view of the truth was flawed. Jesse Washington hung from a tree, roasting over a bonfire for two hours, lowered up and down. He tried to climb the chain, but the mob had cut off his fingers, cut off his balls. I said, "Grandpa, nobody in Africa is swinging from trees."

The *Waco Tribune-Herald* publishes an article upon the 100th anniversary of the lynching. In an online comment, one McLennan County resident writes,

"Jesse Washington got exactly what he deserved. .... If I had been alive at the time I would have gladly participated."

My great-grandfather, James Columbus Russell, married
Bob and Peggy's daughter Dinah in 1909. Jim Russell
was teaching science at the all-black Paul Quinn College
in Waco in 1916, year of the infamous Jesse Washington
lynching. On the Flickr page for Baylor University's
historic Texas Collection, I find five photographs of Paul
Quinn students and faculty taken that year. The name on
the photographs is Gildersleeve, official photographer of
the lynching.

The morning of May 15th,
while Jesse Washington stood
on trial, Gildersleeve set up his
equipment in the mayor's
office overlooking the town
square. Later it was suggested
that the mayor got a cut when
Gildersleeve sold the lynching
postcards as souvenirs.

I keep searching the Paul Quinn photographs for my
great-grandfather's face—bent over a beaker in a chemistry
lab or looming six feet tall in the back row of a group
portrait. Some of the students look somberly at the camera,
but most look away. I can't find Jim Russell anywhere, but
here is a young girl who wears black stockings with white-
strapped slippers instead of boots, a mulatto girl with
messy hair like me, and she's looking right at Gildersleeve.

Somehow I am investigating a lynching. No, I am investigating my family's relationship to a lynching. Here the page brakes.

All the jury find the defendant Guilty
as charged in the indictment
and assess his punishment at death
W. B. Brazelton
Foreman

Courtesy of the McLennan County District Clerk's Office

A jury foreman signs a death sentence and the mob drags the black boy from the kangaroo court to be strung up, beaten, burned, hacked into bits as souvenirs. The foreman complains: the black boy was meant to be murdered by the state.

There's a name in here I've heard before. There was a Mr. Brazelton my grandpa caddied for. He carried Brazelton's clubs, watched him putt. Was it W.B. Brazelton, foreman, or W.B. Brazelton's son?

Mr. Brazelton said to Grandpa, "You're not like those other colored boys," told him to go to college, and later Mr. Brazelton handed Grandpa his first teaching job. Mr. Brazelton was on the school board, or maybe it was Mr. Brazelton's wife—one of them twisted an arm.

I have been drinking in desecrated ways. Fraught in cantankerous jitneys.
I want to garble my fortitude in blue blocks.

"You're not like those other colored boys," Mr. Brazelton said. I was
going to make this page a pantoum, that line cycling through.

The Huguenot must have pronounced his name *Hue-bear.* The Texas Huberts say *Huh-burt*, the first syllable a short "uh" like in "uh huh," an old standby, though its meaning shifts depending on the emphasis. Some of Priscilla's children, Texans to the tailbone, went a step further and changed the spelling to *Hubbard.* But the cousins who moved to California decided *Huh-burt* was "country" and pronounce their name *Hue-burt.* The ones who went to New Orleans are sometimes called *Her-bear,* landing not far off from the Huguenot.

Josh David: I can't tell you the exact truth of the thing. Don't swear it in court.

L. Michael Russell: This is as good a rendition of the facts as any.

When we met Josh David he said, "You didn't think you'd meet a real cowboy when you came. … I'm a cow man. You know the difference between a cowboy and a cow man? Cowboy works for the man owns the cows. Cow man *owns* the cows." Josh David is the great-grandson of Bob Hubert's friend and neighbor Josh David, who gets a lot of ink in Hubert's diary. The modern-day Josh David wears stiff leather cowboy boots and a broad white hat turned up at the brim. He shows us Bob Hubert's new gravesite in the Turner Cemetery. "Why is a Confederate monument sharp?" Josh David quips. "To keep a damn Yankee from setting down on it and resting." He is a keeper of histories, a weaver of tall tales, and likes to tell jokes that have me laughing to one side, my grin veering slightly off kilter.

In 1995 the Sons of Confederate Veterans reburied the remains of Hubert's nephew Captain Ike Turner, who was killed in battle in 1863. Turner was buried back in Georgia, on his family's old plantation, Turnwold, where his body quietly decomposed over the next 130 years until the Sons of Confederate Veterans decided that the Captain's dying wish was for a Texas burial. They equipped the remains with a new casket, which lay in the rotunda of Georgia's Old Governors' Mansion before departing for Texas—an eerie reenactment of Turner's own antebellum journey, one imagines, but this time not by covered wagon. Reports of the reburial ceremonies mention a six-pound cannon named for Ike Turner, as well as a color guard and period brass band, followed by whole companies of Confederate reenactors and ladies in antebellum dress strewing rose petals. At the new gravesite, they all listened to eulogies commemorating Turner's service to the Confederacy.

The newly reorganized Ike Turner Camp of the Sons of Confederate Veterans enjoyed the attention they received for the Turner ceremony, and maybe they were out looking for another hero to bury or maybe they had one more cannon left to dedicate when they tramped into the woods with a backhoe and unearthed Bob Hubert's buttons, a few shards of bone, and replanted his and his wife Jenny's tombstones in the Turner Cemetery with the rest of the white folks. Peggy's grave, unmarked at Bob's feet, they left alone.

When I followed Josh David into the woods, it was Peggy's grave I was after. She was buried sometime between 1894 and 1900 on the old homeplace, what was then Bob Hubert's land, gone to woods now, and one tree is growing sideways out of the earth, extended like a hand. There used to be a cement cover over Peggy's grave. "During the '60s, during Civil Rights, the [white] Huberts claimed the blacks tore it down, but knowing the Huberts it might have been the Huberts tore it all down," Josh David said. "… You can't tell which bunch did it."

Later I learn that in 1964, a Confederate marker was placed on Bob Hubert's grave, at the request of one of his nephews. This was not long after Reverend Bryant Hubert, grandson of Bob and Peggy, was campaigning for LBJ. Is this when the marker disappeared from Peggy's grave?

My Polk County cousins do not know where to find either place. Before the reburial, the Sons of Confederate Veterans never asked permission from any of Bob Hubert's direct descendants. We probably wouldn't have granted it. We are all black, and as the Sons of the Confederate Veterans may have surmised, do not share their nostalgia for the Confederacy.

CEREMONIUM MORTEUM

The Reburial of Captain Robert Wallace Hubert, and His Wife, Jenny, in Loving Memory by the Sons of Confederate Veterans, April 25, 1999

Early Baptist Funeral Service

I.   Introduction and Background

Bob Hubert placed his family
cemetery on the old survey straddling
the county line—where he planned to lie
forever with his black mistress at his feet
and his white wife by his side.

II.   Death and Burial

A backhoe unearthed
buttons in the overgrowth,
a few shards of bone. Who
scooped them up? A backhoe bucking
a black hole.   Who segregated
        the family plot?

III.   Resurrection

Heard a whippoorwill holler. A whimper,
a whistle.   Whipped out
of the woods—a dart
        through the center.

IV.   Collect of the Day—for the Captain Robert Wallace Hubert Scholarship Fund

God the Father, bless these gifts and have mercy on your servant Bob, who sent his daughters to school—Wiley College, Prairie View—*said he didn't want them working in no white man's kitchen, 'cause he knew*—that he may share with you through your Son, our Lord, who was once human too.   Amen.

V.   The Dismissal—Pass by the Caskets
    for the Last Respects

passed on   passed through
    passed into   passed beyond
passing (present participle):   crossing over
        to never come back

High Military Service for the Dead

I.   Receiving the Deceased

No one will say
what happened to the marker
on Peggy's grave, the cement
cover Bob or their children laid.

II.   The Procession

Even in death, Rebels can fall
perfectly into step. There is Major
Jimmy Littlefield, the quartermaster,
and barefoot John Stevens, following
the bagpipers. And Bob's
nephew Ike—recently reburied, still
twenty-four, still dashing
and dying in his uniform—winks
at Bob and says, "It's only matter."

III.   Blessing of the Cannon
        Named for Capt. Hubert

Bless this cannon
with its rebel name. Expect
an expansive range. It shoots
straight, but don't forget to aim.

IV.   The Graveside Services

Into the ground we commend
these buttons. Button up what can't be
shucked. What goes down must come up.

V.   The Internment
        Dismissal of the Artillerymen

The Houston Highlander Bagpipe Band
"Amazing Grace"

Hubert Family Re-Union, and Picnic-on-th
Grounds! (Excluding direct descendants,
some colors out of bounds.)

CAPTAIN ROBERT WALLACE HUBERT
COMPANY K, 5TH TEXAS INFANTRY
HOOD'S BRIGADE

"In Loving Memory"

HIS BELOVED WIFE
VIRGINIA A. (JENNY) DUNCAN

CEREMONIUM MORTEUM

INTRODUCTION AND RECOGNITION OF GUESTS
CAMP ADJUTANT, CHRIS D. PARKER

EULOGY - CAMP COMMANDER, MACK E. NEAL, Col

EARLY BAPTIST CHURCH FUNERAL SERVICE
CAMP CHAPLIN, JAMES N. HENDRIX

I. INTRODUCTION AND BACKGROUND

SONG - "TRINITY" BLUEGRASS GOSPEL BAND

II. DEATH AND BURIAL

SONG - "TRINITY" BLUEGRASS GOSPEL BAND

III. RESURRECTION

SONG - "TRINITY" BLUEGRASS GOSPEL BAND

IV. THE COLLECT OF THE DAY - FOR THE CAPTAIN
ROBERT WALLACE HUBERT SCHOLARSHIP FUND

V. THE DISMISSAL - PASS BY THE CASKETS FOR THE
LAST RESPECTS

THE HOUSTON HIGHLANDER BAGPIPE BAND

FORM UP FOR THE PROCESSIONAL

CEREMONIUM MORTEUM

ANGLICAN-EPISCOPALIAN - METHODIST - SOUTH
HIGH MILITARY SERVICE FOR THE DEAD

REV. D. PRESLEY HUTCHENS, AND ACOLYTES

I. RECEIVING THE DECEASED

II. THE PROCESSION
THE HOUSTON HIGHLANDER BAGPIPE BAND

III. BLESSING OF THE CANNONS - DEDICATION OF
THE CANNON NAMED FOR CAPT. HUBERT

IV. THE GRAVESIDE SERVICES

V. THE INTERMENT - LOWERING OF THE CASKETS
THE HOUSTON HIGHLANDER BAGPIPE BAND
"AMAZING GRACE"

DISMISSAL OF THE ARTILLERYMEN

AWARD OF THE CONFEDERATE, "SOUTHER CROSS OF
HONOR" TO MAJOR RON STEINFELS

DEDICATION OF THE TEXAS STATE HISTORICAL
MARKER

INFANTRYMEN RIFLE VOLLEYS - THREE

"THE CANNONADE" - TWENTY-ONE GUN SALUTE

COVERING OF THE GRAVES

HUBERT FAMILY RE-UNION, AND PICNIC-ON-THE
GROUNDS!

Two years after our adventure with Josh David, I stumble upon a 1999 newspaper article announcing Robert Wallace Hubert's reburial. Although by now none of this should be surprising, I'm enraged when I read the fourth paragraph: "Virginia, Captain Hubert's wife, died as a result of childbirth, and he lamented her death and never remarried for the remainder of his life." I wonder what Peggy would have to say—or any of Bob's many children. It is true that Bob grieved his wife's early death for the rest of his life. Five months before his own death, he wrote, "Fifty seven years have passed and yet the grief is still strong. Nobody knows but myself how strong and deep." It is true that Bob Hubert never remarried. Neither did Thomas Jefferson, but by 1999 we had all heard of Sally Hemings.

I came to this project in search of Peggy, but it is my life, too, my family's life, I find expunged from the record.

Captain Hubert to be reburied in Confederate style April 25

LIVINGSTON – Captain Robert Wallace Hubert will be reburied in Confederate Style on April 25 by the Ike Turner Camp 1275, Sons of Confederate Veterans.

Since the Texas Senate has adopted State Resolution 526, on March 30, recognizing April as "Confederate History and Heritage Month," the Ike Turner Chapter has planned several events during the weekend of the re-burial of Captain Robert Wallace Hubert, of Company K, 5th Texas Infantry, and his wife, Virginia A. "Jenny" Duncan Hubert.

Captain Hubert was the uncle of the Camp's namesake, Captain Ike Turner, and was instrumental in forming the Company when it was organized in August of 1861.

Virginia, Captain Hubert's wife, died as a result of childbirth, and he lamented her death and never remarried for the remainder of his life.

After his death Feb. 7, 1917, he was buried on his farm in Polk County. Throughout the years with the land changing ownership several times and with all the timbering activities, his grave was lost several times. After 50 years, the grave was rediscovered in 1992 by Leon Dickens back in the timberlands of Polk County.

In 1998, the Captain Ike Turner 1275 Camp, Sons of Confederate Veterans, was able to cut a road into the area. On Oct. 12, 1998, with the help of heavy equipment that could be brought into the area, the bodies of Captain Hubert and his wife Virginia were exhumed. Their remains were transferred to Cochran Funeral Home in Livingston to await the reburial at the J.A.S. Turner Family Cemetery.

The reburial will be Sunday, April 25, at 11 a.m. A church service will be held under a tent on the farm of Leon Dickens in the Midway community, followed by the processional and reburial at the J.A.S. Turner Cemetery, which is adjacent to the farm, and a 21-Gun Cannon Salute. Everyone is invited to the re-burial, which is a live event and not a reenactment.

The Captain Ike Turner Camp is planning the re-burial to follow as closely as possible, all of the things that might have been experienced in the 1860s.

The schedule of events is as follows:

Saturday April 24
2 p.m. Ladies Lemonade Social
3 p.m. Live Musket Shoot
6 p.m. Supper Hour
7 p.m. Dance-on-the-Grounds
9 p.m. The Rites of St. Barbara
Sunday, April 25
8 to 10 a.m. Lying-In-State
10 to 11 a.m. Dulcimer string band plays in the church tent
11 a.m. Church Services, and paying last respects.
noon – Procession to the cemetery, horse-drawn, glass window hearse.
12:30 p.m. Form up at cemetery and begin dedication of the new Texas State Historical Marker, and award to Major Ron Steinfels of the "Confederate Cross of Honor."
12:45 p.m. Graveside services, firing of the rifle volleys, and a 21-gun cannonade. Lowering of the caskets, while the bagpipers play "Amazing Grace." Covering the graves.
1 p.m. Hubert-Turner Family Reunion with a picnic-on-the-Grounds.

The public is invited to view any of these events.

All customs, ceremonies and dress shall be of the 1860s period. This is not required of the family and spectators.

To get to the Leon Dickens Farm, travel east from Livingston on U.S. Highway 190, 24.5 miles from the courthouse, across Little Hickory Creek. Several green cemetery signs will be on the left, turn here to your left. Go 2 miles north to the fork in the road, go right, you will see Leon Dickens farm cattleguard in front of you.

This event is being hosted by the Captain Ike Turner Camp 1275, Sons of the Confederate Veterans, the Ike Turner Chapter 1569, United Daughters of the Confederacy, and the Magnolia Chapter, Order of the Confederate Rose.

LHS to perform One-Act Play

LIVINGSTON -- The One-Act Play cast and crew of Livingston High School will hold a free performance of Horton Foote's "The Trip to Bountiful" at 3 p.m. Sunday, April 25, in the high school auditorium.

The public is invited, as this is the group's way of saying thank you to the community for all their support.

CONFEDERATE REBURIAL -- The Captain Ike Turner Camp 1275, Sons of the Confederate Veterans proceeds to the J.A.S. Turner Family Cemetery for the reburial of Captain Robert Wallace Hubert and his wife Virginia A. "Jenny" Duncan on Sunday, April 25. Also participating in the event was the Ike Turner Chapter 1569, United Daughters of the Confederacy and the Magnolia Chapter, Order of the Confederate Rose. The reburial was planned to follow as closely as possible all of the things that might have been experienced in the 1860s.

The photographer's walls are papered with tintypes. There are women in crisp new collars, shiny buttons climbing in rows nearly to their throats. One woman, barely more than a girl, wears three carnations pinned to her dress, and if it weren't for the vaguely delineated petals you would almost mistake the carnations for cotton just plucked from the boll. There are men with manicured beards, bewildered-looking children, and one infant who couldn't have lived even a year, lying motionless on a curved black sofa, eyes closed, her coral necklace painstakingly tinted pink. Bob is fixated on this photograph, and later when he sits for the portrait, it is this he will be thinking of—not the living boy Plunk beside him nor the cedar tree he planted at his wife's grave nor the Fifth New York Zouaves at Second Manassas with their red blouse pants, how so many lay dead and wounded on the ground that afterward General Hill said the battlefield looked like a bed of roses. No, he will be thinking of the two small coffins he built in the years just before the war, the sticky August heat and the heft of the saw through cedar wood. And then Plunk will say "Sir?" or is it "Papa?" and he will look up, hearing the photographer whistle a song Jenny used to sing during her second, fatal pregnancy, a song he'd thought he heard on Peggy's lips once only, just after his return. Then the whistling will stop, and the photographer will emerge from behind the camera, with one hand raising the black cloth.

Courtesy of the late Bryant Hubert

Your Results

Scandinavia	Western and Central Africa	Great Britain and Ireland	Southern Europe	Asia Minor	Jewish Diaspora	Southern Africa
36%	32%	15%	10%	3%	2%	2%

When the Genographic Project says I am more Scandinavian than African, I don't know how to feel about it. If I went to Denmark in this skin, this smoking cyclone crown of frizz, and declared the findings, who would they convince?

I'm told I am more Scandinavian than African and wonder where this belongs in the half-built book I am no longer living in. Bob Hubert was always gathering moss for the mud cat chimneys he raised over Polk County. A county surveyor knew where lines bent. Did he leave behind a genetic map? "Bob came through and made everybody kin," one of my cousins laughs.

From Emma Haynes's *History of Polk County*, 1937:

asked that they wait and for him have a chance to whip him.
When Gordon's term was out and he was leaving the county, Stevens
caught ..... near Swan..st and beat him nearly to death.
The people .. the South .. .. ..ore respect for General Grant
than they did for Abraham Lincoln. A picture of Lincoln was
not allowed in the house.
A Union camp was also .... at Moscow. The people
round about suffered, for the soldiers burned cotton, corn ..
..... and at .... Towns remembers that one
day one of his .... .. ex-slaves went into the house with a
grieved .... of his face, holding a handful of seed cotton,
and in a mournful .. he said "Miss..dis all we got." The Yankees
had burned their gin and cotton. They left one hog down for
that family to eat.
When the camp was established at Moscow every house was closed,
and negroes paraded up and down the streets. The next morning
four negroes were found hanging to a tree. The KuKlux Klan
would control the negros, and did to a great extent; but the
citizens were kept in constant fear of a negro uprising.
It seems that residents of Polk County were allowed to run
one parts of .... if they had not held office
in the Confederate Army. Some of the officers during this
time were John R. Johnson, (... been a surveyor), .. J. Galloway,
Manton Marsh and J... Cater. The jurors at one time in 1868
were men who had fought in the war. However, negroes were
deprived for about four months, and after that the citizens
had a sheriff; but he was not allowed to do his duty, and neither
did the Union soldiers keep .. .. so that much crime was done.
Moscow had been known as a .. .. .. that always cooperated well
in everything; but this period of reconstruction did much
to bring about disruption, and .... five years recovering
the group spirit. Moscow and Livingston were quite rough during
and shortly after this period.
The union soldiers and ... . were kept in Polk County
about two years, 1866-68. .... the people suffered they
escaped much that people farther east endured. The news that most
people were treated better .. .... and brought settlers to this
county.
Oh, that people loved peace rather than war!

In the book I built where I no longer live:

Some nights humming's in the walls. Not
wind hissing through chinks but a human
song that shifts in sleep and dips
into a low diphthong—

After the fellowship year, I stay in Madison—not because I like it (I don't), but because I have nowhere in particular to go. I make friends. In the fall I get a part-time job tutoring student athletes at the University of Wisconsin and a second part-time job at the Wisconsin Historical Society, supervising teenage interns as they work on African American history projects. I'm not making enough money, really, to continue to pay my bills, so in January I will add teaching a documentary poetics workshop to my list of part-time gigs. There are days when I roll out of bed at noon and meet a friend in a coffee shop to fiddle around in our respective notebooks, and there are ten- and twelve-hour days when I rush on foot, windblown, from job to job. Often I feel desperate and lonely. But even in this I have some control. I own my own body: my hands, my hips, my cunt, my unruly black and white curls frizzing in the wind. And out of my loneliness I am making—what?

I read an article in *The Atlantic* that claims lonely elderly people may be more susceptible to inflammation and less able to fight off infection than their less isolated peers. An article in the *Huffington Post* suggests that we younger lonely are no better off and that in fact loneliness is predictive of early death. The title of the *Huffington Post* article is "Loneliness Can Kill, Literally." I can recognize the melodrama, the title's clickbait appeal, but I nonetheless swallow the article I already feel, intuitively, to be true. At times my loneliness has felt like an overgrown vine, kudzu strangling me with its many limbs. My last autumn in New York, in the midst of an excruciating loneliness that lasted for months, I heard an opera singer interviewed on NPR. I can't remember her name. She said she used to be terrified of loneliness, until a famous composer told her,

"Loneliness gives us space to create." I can't say that when
I heard this I tore the vine from my neck or severed any of
its too-tenacious limbs. But periodically, for years at a time,
I stopped wrestling it and we two would coexist—not like
lovers but like the brokenness that love becomes, which is a
troubled kind of peace. At the bottom of my loneliness I see
a rope swinging overhead, sometimes dipping into the well.
"It is a noose," warns Peggy. "No, a ladder," Bob says.

What is home with none to meet,
None to welcome, none to greet us;
Home is sweet, and only sweet,
Where there's one who loves to meet us!

I don't know it yet, but in the spring I will get a job as the
assistant director of a new center for black poetry back in
Pittsburgh, where I won't feel like such an anomaly walking
down the street. Donald Trump will be nominated for
President, running on a surge of white hatred and fear. Every
other week, it seems, a video of police shooting an unarmed
black person will go viral. The tension is pervasive: The
Confederate flag tee-shirt at the Fourth of July fireworks
display, the "All Lives Matter" contingent drowning out
Queers for Racial Equity at my last Madison pride parade.
Sometimes the tension will feel almost solid, and I can
imagine John Brown hacking into it with his broadsword,
Nat Turner's band with their axes and scythes.

At the Democratic National Convention that summer,
Michelle Obama will speak of the "story of generations of
people who felt the lash of bondage, the shame of servitude,
the sting of segregation, but who kept on striving and

hoping and doing what needed to be done so that today I wake up every morning in a house that was built by slaves. And I watch my daughters—two beautiful, intelligent, black young women—playing with their dogs on the White House lawn."

There will be a backlash on my Facebook feed. A young black scholar I know posts that Michelle Obama has no sense of history. "Last time I checked slaves were not protesting—or fighting for their lives—to sleep in the White House. Actually I have found no definitive record stating that chattel slaves imagined freedom and liberation by way of sleeping in the White House (i.e. the slave master's house). ... Michelle's speech was not only a misreading of our past, but equally damaging to our possibility to imagine freedom in the future."

But when I hear the speech, I will feel a jolt of recognition. There are days when I am sitting at my desk at the Center for African American Poetry and Poetics, housed in the University of Pittsburgh's forty-two-story gothic Cathedral of Learning, a "master's house" built to distinguish who is in from who is out, when I will wonder, "What would Peggy think of this?" I will know it is not the right question, that I am living in a world Peggy could not possibly imagine. This is a way of speaking to the past without ever actually conversing with it.

The winter before I leave Madison, I will fall in love with a close friend. Eventually she will get a good job in Pittsburgh and follow me there, but by the time she arrives, we will have fallen out of love. On the first day of fall, two days after we break up, my no-longer love will drive a U-Haul from

Madison to Pittsburgh, and I will sit in my office imagining my heart pulverized, or stabbed through the right ventricle, and I will know it is beginning to mend. I know my Peggy is no approximation of the real Peggy, but the Peggy I know can see me here with my broken heart, and holds me, for a moment, still—whether or not she believes we can transform the master's house from within.

—Madison, December 19, 2015
Pittsburgh, September 22, 2016

Peggy:

That moon ain't hiding—cloud's a shawl. Moon's cold
as brass, tacked upside night's frock. Pin your tears
to her, they'll sing like chimes. Or ghosts that cry,
Sometimes I feel I'm ah–almost gone—
ghosts charred in dead men's lust. Think I'm some fool
got brains of shucks? Since freedom I been through
the toughs. See, one moon casts your shadow twice:
once toward the bottomland, once toward the pines.
The wind's right smart, but moon, she sly. Look: Light-
ning bugs, they spark, but they cannot catch fire.

Notes

I am a poet. I am not a historian.

In the summer of 2013, I acquired a copy of Robert Wallace Hubert's 1889-1894 and 1917 diaries from the Polk County Historical Museum and Historical and Genealogical Library. Over the next year I transcribed all 225 pages. Through that process, I became increasingly interested in Hubert's omissions and decided to write into the space of what is missing. Thus this book is the product of a particular imagination but an imagination instigated by encounters with Hubert's diaries and with texts of all sorts, both primary and secondary, which provide the bedrock of facts, myths, perspectives, memories, images, turns of phrase, and silences from which creation springs. Though compiling a comprehensive list may be impossible, most of those texts are listed below.

I am grateful to everyone who generously shared their memories, photographs, records, and understanding of events with me, listed separately under Acknowledgements. I also owe much to the stories of my grandfather, Lewis V. Russell, some of which I compiled in a biographical pamphlet as a thirteen-year-old, nine years before his death at age ninety-six. My grandfather was also the source of the strange story of the slave and the white man who fell into a well.

In the introduction, the sentence "I am writing into the silences, the omissions, what has been left out either intentionally or because by its nature it defies legibility" echoes a prompt Dawn Lundy Martin gave our graduate workshop in 2013, which includes the language, "Consider for a moment not what is left behind, but what is never spoken or made visible—either deliberately or because it resists visibility. Write toward this absence while considering its relationship to history and your body?" In style and perhaps spirit, the introduction is influenced by Eleni Sikelianos's marvelous opening to *The Book of Jon*.

*Note on "Head-quarters, District of Texas": This substitution poem took a curious turn when I realized that only the first two paragraphs of the "transcription" I was using are the actual text of the Texas Emancipation (Juneteenth) Proclamation, General Gordon Granger's General Order No. 3. The paragraphs "2nd," "3rd" and "4th" appear only in an online "transcription" I discovered was fictitious after I obtained a scan of the original document from the Dallas Historical Society. But perhaps it is not *completely* fictitious, since "2nd," "3rd," and "4th," do contain some sentiments—though not the exact language—found in General Granger's subsequent "circular" published in Texas newspapers in the weeks following Juneteenth. Since this is not a work of history but of biomythology, and the false transcription extends the imaginative possibilities of the original, I decided to leave the poem as it stands. "Peggies" is substituted for "slaves," "readbeard(s) for "employer(s)," "Robert(s) for "owner(s)" and "master(s)," "song" for "contract," "whippoorwill" for "laborer" and "whippoorwilling" for "labor," "blue bandanna" for "employee," and "black bottom(s)" for "freedman/men."

I consulted a number of primary sources in addition to Robert Wallace Hubert's diaries.

Among these are unpublished family photographs and documents. Other genealogical materials include the United States Census, archived at the National Archives and Records Administration and available online through Ancestry.com; Texas Death Certificates, 1903-1982, from the Texas Department of State Health Services and available online through Ancestry.com; the Will of Benjamin B. Hubert, in Warren County, Georgia, Will Book 1 (1798-1808), archived at the Washington Memorial Library in Macon, Georgia; the marriage record for Louisa Perryman and Lucias Tharpe, archived at Sam Houston Regional Library and Research Center, Texas State Library and Archives Commission; Georgia Property Tax Digests and the State Census of North Carolina 1784-1787, both available online through Ancestry.com; and J.A.S. Turner's service records for both the Mexican War and the Florida (Second Seminole) War, archived at the National Archives and accessible online through Fold3. Some of Bob and Peggy's daughters are listed in Wiley University yearbooks, accessible online through The University of North Texas Libraries' Portal to Texas History.

Robert W. Hubert's Confederate service records are stored at the National Archives Building in Washington, D.C., and may also be found online through Fold3. On the activities of Hood's Texas Brigade and particularly Company K, William A. Fletcher's memoir *Rebel Private: Front and Rear Memoirs of a Confederate Soldier*, originally published in 1908 and reprinted in 2011, was useful, as was John W. Stevens's *Reminiscences of the Civil War: Life in Hood's Texas Brigade, Army of Northern Virginia*, first published in 1902 and republished in 2016 by Endeavor Press Ltd. Also helpful were Decimus et Ultimus Barziza's memoir *The Adventures of a Prisoner of War 1863-1864*, originally published in 1865 and republished by the University of Texas Press in 1964. Documentation of Hood's Texas Brigade was compiled in General Jerome B. Robertson's *Touched with Valor: Civil War Papers and Casualty Reports of Hood's Texas Brigade*, edited by Harold B. Simpson and published by Hill Junior College Press in 1964. For a Union perspective, I also looked at Joshua Lawrence Chamberlain's field report on the defense of Little Round Top at Gettysburg, available through *The War of the Rebellion: A Compilation of the Official Records of the Union And Confederate Armies,* which can be accessed online through University of North Texas Libraries, The Portal to Texas History, via UNT Libraries Government Documents Department. The startling image of the dead at Second Manassas is from Bob Hubert's diary. Near the end of his life, he remembered, "I have heard it said that Gen Hill made the remark that the battle ground looked like a bed of roses, so many of the Zouaves were killed and wounded and left on the battle field."

The Federal Writers Project's oral histories of former slaves in Texas, conducted in the 1930s, were published in Volumes 4 and 5 of *The American Slave: A Composite Autobiography*, compiled by George P. Rawick. These are also now available online through the Library of Congress. *I Was Born in Slavery: Personal Accounts of Slavery in Texas*, edited by Andrew Waters and published in 2003 by John F. Blair, is a more manageable size, containing twenty-eight selections from the Federal Writers Project's Texas narratives. Actual sound recordings of interviews with former slaves, including Harriet Smith and Bob Ledbetter, are available online from the Library of Congress's *American Memory*. Also invaluable were *Women's Slave Narratives*, collected and published by

Dover, and Harriet Jacobs' *Incidents in the Life of a Slave Girl, Written by Herself,* edited by Nell Irvin Painter and published by Penguin.

I took some language from the oral histories and put it in Peggy's mouth, including "Since Freedom, I's been through the toughs," from Rosina Howard (spelled "Hoard" in the earlier transcription), and "the burst of freedom come in June," from Sarah Ashley, whose oral histories from the Federal Writers Project are both included in *I Was Born in Slavery: Personal Accounts of Slavery in Texas.* Adeline Marshall, whose "no nation" statement is quoted in the Jesse Hubbard section, remembered "red russet shoes" that "pizen the feet." Her first name is transcribed as "Adeline" by the Federal Writers Project and as "Adline" in the *Born in Slavery* edition later edited by Andrew Waters. In an audio recording of an interview conducted by John Henry Faulk, Harriet Smith remembered singing "Are We Born To Die?" in church, but I initially misheard it as "We Born To Die." Several of the narrators recalled being brought to Texas by ox-drawn wagon. Josephine Howard remembered, "Us and the women am put in the wagons, but the men slaves am chained together and has to walk," and this detail was so piercing that I paraphrased it for Peggy's recollection, though not all of the accounts of forced relocation to Texas describe enslaved men making the trek in chains. I have no way of knowing if Bob Hobert chained men for the journey, but I *want* to believe what seems to me an equally likely if not likelier possibility, that he did not.

The Polk County Enterprise (Livingston, Tex.), 1907-1913, edited by E. J. Manry, & W. L. West, can be accessed through the University of North Texas Libraries, The Portal to Texas History, via Livingston Municipal Library.

*Proceedings of the State Convention of Colored Men of Texas,
Held at The City of Austin, July 10-12, 1883*, compiled by
I.B. Scott, Secretary, was printed in Houston in 1883 by
Smallwood & Gray, Steam Printers.

The Texas Emancipation Proclamation (General Gordon
Granger's General Order No. 3.) is archived at the Dallas
Historical Society.

Fred Gildersleeve's 1916 photographs of students
and faculty at Paul Quinn College are archived in the
Gildersleeve-DuConge Collection of the Texas Collection
at Baylor University and can be accessed online through The
Texas Collection, Baylor University Flickr. Gildersleeve's
photographs of the horrendous lynching of Jesse
Washington have been widely disseminated and appeared
in *The Crisis* only months later, thanks to the early efforts
of Elisabeth Freeman and W.E.B. DuBois. "The Waco
Horror," an eight-page supplement to the July, 1916 issue
of *The Crisis*, is available online through the Modernist
Journals Project, a joint project of Brown University and the
University of Tulsa. Oral histories collected by the Baylor
University Institute for Oral History are available online in
the project "Legacy of Jesse Washington Lynching." Harold
Lester Goodman's eyewitness account, captured on audio
in 1977, is also available through the Baylor University
Institute for Oral History and was republished by the *Waco
Herald-Tribune.* The verdict, signed by jury foreman W.B.
Brazelton, is archived at the McLennan County District
Clerk's Office. I believe the Brazelton my grandfather
caddied for was probably *not* W.B. Brazelton but his son,
Thomas Berry Brazelton, Sr., father of the well-known
pediatrician T. Berry Brazelton, whose memoir *Learning to*

Listen: A Life of Caring for Children confirms that his father had liberal views on race by Waco standards and that his mother was on the schoolboard.

The text of several articles on Jesse Hubbard appear in this book: "Hubbard in Form," *The Gazette*, Cleveland, OH, August 14, 1920; "No-Run No-Hit Game," *Philadelphia Inquirer*, July 17, 1919; "Jesse Hubbard in Hero Act," published in *The Pittsburgh Courier*, July 2, 1938, with a byline credited to Harry Levette, accessed through ProQuest Historical Newspapers. Minutes of the State of Texas vs. Jess Hubert are archived at the Sam Houston Regional Library and Research Center, Texas State Library and Archives Commission.

Barbara White covered the 1999 reburial of Robert Wallace Hubert's remains in *The Polk County Enterprise*, accessed online through the University of North Texas Libraries, The Portal to Texas History, via Livingston Municipal Library. The 1995 reburial of Bob Hubert's nephew Ike Turner is described in detail in Randy Hill's article "A Southern Homecoming," published in usadeepsouth.com, and preceding the event, by Barbara White in *The Polk County Enterprise*.

Among the many secondary sources I consulted, the most essential were:

Genealogical materials including Sarah Donelson's *Genealogy of the Family of Benjamin B. Hubert, A Huguenot*, printed in Atlanta in 1897 by Franklin Printing and Publishing, Lester F. Russell's *Profile of a Black Heritage*, printed by Graphicopy in Franklin Square, New York, in 1977, and Willa Mann's unpublished genealogy of Huberts descended from Dinah Alford.

On antebellum slavery and its aftermath, I referenced Herbert C. Gutman's *The Black Family in Slavery and Freedom 1750-1925*, published by Pantheon in 1976; Wilma King's article "'Prematurely Knowing of Evil Things': The Sexual Abuse of African American Girls and Young Women in Slavery and Freedom" published in *The Journal of African American History*, 99.3, in 2014; and Deborah Gray White's *Ar'nt I A Woman? Female Slaves in the Plantation South*, published by Norton in 1985. For the kinds of minute details that make poetry, I also consulted Helen Bradley Foster's *"New Raiments of Self": African American Clothing in the Antebellum South*, published by Berg in 1997, and Patricia B. Mitchell's self-published *Plantation Row Slave Cabin Cooking: The Roots of Soul Food*, published in 1998.

On Polk County, Texas: Norma Hammond McLoughlin's *Deep Roots in the Tall Pines: A History of Polk County, Texas*, published in 2006 by McLoughlin Publishers, provides many useful particulars about daily life in Polk County in Bob and Peggy's day. Also essential were Emma R. Haynes's *The History of Polk County*, first printed in 1937 and republished by the Polk County Historical Commission in 1996; *A Pictorial History of Polk County, Texas (1846-1910)*, published by the Polk County Bicentennial Commission in 1976; and Richard B. McCaslin's entry on Polk County in the Texas Historical Association's *Handbook of Texas Online*.

For a general overview of Texas history, I consulted two books called *Texas: An Illustrated History*, one by David G.

McComb published by Oxford University Press in 1995 and one by John Perry published by Hippocrene Books in 2011. For more information about the Alabama-Coushatta Tribe's history in Texas, I read Howard N. Martin's article "Alabama-Coushatta Indians" and W.E.S. Dickerson's article "Indian Relations," both in the Texas Historical Association's *Handbook of Texas Online*. To understand the history of land acquisition in the nineteenth century, I referred to the PDF *History of Texas Public Lands*, published by the Texas General Land Office in 1992 and now available through the website of the Texas Board of Professional Land Surveying in Texas.

There are two overlapping resources on the Georgia Military Institute: Gary Livingston's *Cradled in Glory: Georgia Military Institute 1851-1865*, published by Caisson Press in 1997, and Bowling C. Yates's earlier *History of the Georgia Military Institute*, published in pamphlet form in Marietta, Georgia in 1968. Both include the 1853 class rankings and conduct roll.

Secondary sources on Hood's Texas Brigade in the Civil War include Harold B. Simpson's *Hood's Texas Brigade: A Compendium*, published by Hill Jr. College Press, 1977; Edward B. Williams's *Hood's Texas Brigade in the Civil War*, published by McFarland & Company in 2012. On the Fifth Texas in particular, I consulted Ruth Peebles's *There Never Were Such Men Before: The Civil War Soldiers and Veterans of Polk County, Texas, 1861-1865*, published by Polk County Historical Commission in 1987, and Brian C. Pohanka's article "Destruction of the 5th New York Zouaves," on the Fifth Texas's role in Second Manassas, available online through American Battlefield Trust. On the assault and defense of Little Round Top at Gettysburg, I referred to Glenn W. LaFantasie's *Twilight at Little Round Top*, published by John Wiley and Sons in 2005. For sensory details, I was lucky to discover Mark M. Smith's *The Smell of Battle, the Taste of Siege: A Sensory History of the Civil War*, published by Oxford University Press in 2015.

The Johnson's Island's Preservation Society's webpage "Depot of Prisoners of War on Johnson's Island, Ohio" is a helpful resource on the prisoner of war camp, especially alongside Barziza's memoir.

On the migration of African Americans from Texas and Louisiana to Los Angeles during World War II, I referred to an online article published by the National Park Service's National Register of Historic Places, "Historic Resources Associated with African Americans in Los Angeles."

Patricia Bernstein's book *The First Waco Horror: The Lynching of Jesse Washington and the Rise of the NAACP* is a well-researched account of the lynching and its consequences. It was published by Texas A&M University Press in 2005. J.B. Smith's article "Waco Horror at 100: Why Jesse Washington's Lynching Still Matters" appeared in *Waco Tribune-Herald* on May 15, 2016, and can be accessed online (with its revealing comments section); Kurt Terry's article "Jesse Washington Lynching" appears online in the *Waco History* website from Baylor University.

On Jesse Hubbard and the history of Negro League Baseball, John Holway's two books were a great resource: *Blackball Stars: Negro League Pioneers*, published by Meckler in 1988, and especially the "Jesse 'Mountain' Hubbard" chapter of *Black Giants*, a condensed version of Holway's 1972 interviews with the ballplayer (unfortunately the original recordings have disappeared), published by Lord Fairfax Press in 2010. Two helpful online resources are the Negro Leagues Baseball Museum's *eMuseum* and the Center for Negro League Baseball Research. The language in the Jesse Hubbard pantoum on page 57 is derived from Jesse's language as presented in *Black Giants*, but I removed fragments from their original context and remixed them. "He'd grip the ball tight and bug his eyes," a marvelous image, is actually referring to another Negro League pitcher. Jesse confirms Ty Cobb's racist reputation:

> *The team that wanted me real bad was the Tigers. But they didn't sign me, because Ty Cobb was there, and he didn't like colored no kind of way. Me and Cobb would have been fighting every day.*

> *Cobb was down in San Diego, playing with Chief Meyers' team in 1919, but he wouldn't play against us. He was taking batting practice, saw us coming in the ballpark, and he went in the clubhouse, changed his clothes, and sat out the game. He was a mean man.*

For more about racial inequity in Madison, Wisconsin, see *The Race to Equity: A Baseline Report on the State of Racial Disparities in Dane County*, published by The Wisconsin Council on Children and Families in 2013. The project was directed by Erica Nelson. My last Madison pride parade, when I marched with Madison Queers and Allies for Racial Equity and a contingent of white onlookers tried to drown us out with "All Lives Matter" chants, was actually in August of 2015, the summer *before* Trump won the Republican Presidential nomination, though he was certainly already running.

The two *Smithsonian* articles I referenced are Sean M. Carrol's "No Year's Eve?" and Tony Horwitz's "PTSD: The Civil War's Hidden Legacy," both published in the January 2015 issue. I also referenced Leeat Granek's article in the *Huffington Post* in April 2015, "Loneliness Can Kill, Literally," and Jessica and Tim Lahey's December 2015 article in *The Atlantic*, "How Loneliness Wears on the Body." The line "I have heard the mermaids singing, each to each" is from T.S. Eliot's poem "The Love Song of J. Alfred Prufrock." The 2016 Facebook post quoted on page 94 is from Cherod Johnson. The image "the pain that opens the door," from Simone Weil's notebooks, was gifted to me by Rita Mae Reese as part of a sonnet crown project—only my "sonnet" was meant to be a prose poem.

Three very different books of remembrance inform my thinking/making: M. NourbeSe Philip's *Zong!*, published by Wesleyan University Press in 2008; Saidiya Hartman's *Lose Your Mother: A Journey Along the Atlantic Slave Route*, published by Farrar, Straus and Giroux in 2007; and Tony Hortwitz's *Confederates in the Attic: Dispatches from the Unfinished Civil War*, published by Vintage Random House in 1998. Horwitz's Trump-era update, "After Charlottesville, New Shades of Gray in a Changing South," appeared in *The Wall Street Journal* on August 25, 2017. How I imagine Peggy exercising her creativity, within the confines of her life, is informed by Alice Walker's essay "In Search of Our Mothers' Gardens," which first appeared in *Ms. Magazine* in 1974.

As a child with undiagnosed autism spectrum disorder, I spent many hours watching and rewatching Ken Burn's PBS series *The Civil War*. In Episode Five, which includes an arresting though perhaps less-than-totally-accurate account of the Battle of Gettysburg, I was most fascinated by the assault and defense of Little Round Top. It was many years before I learned that my great-great-grandfather had participated in the attack.

Further resources that contributed to the development of this work include the Bullock Texas State History Museum in Austin, Texas; Gettysburg National Military Park in Gettysburg, Pennsylvania; Heritage Village Museum in Woodville, Texas; the Polk County Memorial Museum in Livingston, Texas; the Wisconsin Veterans Museum, including interactive battle maps from the Civil War Trust; and two African American Genealogy conferences organized by the Wisconsin Historical Society: Strategies and Stories in 2014, and African American Genealogy: Telling Your Story in 2015.

ACKNOWLEDGMENTS

Selections from this book, sometimes in earlier iterations, appear in *Boog City, The Brooklyn Rail, Cream City Review, Hyperallergic, Positive Magnets,* Jaded Ibis Press's *Scarlet,* The Academy of American Poets' *Poem-a-Day, Notre Dame Review, The Tiny,* the anthology *Furious Flower: Seeding the Future of African American Poetry* from Northwestern University Press, the anthology *Show Us Your Papers* from Main Street Rag, and in a limited-edition broadside from Oxeye Press. Thanks to Lauren Alleyne, Anselm Berrigan, Daniela Buccilli, Jordan Dunn, David Kirschenbaum, Dawn Lundy Martin, John Mulrooney, Gina Myers, Wendy Scott Paff, Joe Pan, Soham Patel, Cherise A. Pollard, Collin Schuster, Allesandra Simmons, Naima Yael Tokunow, Steve Tomasula, Gabriella Torres, and Tobias Wray for your faith in this hybrid work, and thanks to the design staff of all those publications for their care with the formatting. "Heard a whippoorwill…," which originally appeared in *The Brooklyn Rail,* was republished on the website of the National Endowment for the Arts.

This book would not have happened without the support of many people.

First of all, my family, the descendants: Thank you to my brother, David Russell, for setting me on the trail of Bob Hubert's diary nearly a decade ago. In Los Angeles, thanks to my parents L. Michael Russell and Lynn Hall Russell, who cheerfully accepted the idea of a family research trip to East Texas. My mother read every installment of Hubert's diary over the year I transcribed it, and as a research assistant in everything but name, her zeal sometimes surpassed my own. In Inglewood, thanks to the late Bryant Hubert, who provided essential information and put us in touch with our Polk County cousins. Thanks to the Texas and Louisiana relatives I met through this work—for your stories, your patience, your hospitality, and your support for the project: Ralph Figgs, James Robert Hubert, the late John Hubert, Linda Stephens, Judy Barlow, Angus Darden, Jennifer Mayo, Ron Darden, and Diana Hubert, and the late Mary Zina Williams. To the relatives I've met only online who were nonetheless essential to this work, I offer my appreciation: Sheryl Powell, Brenda Swearingen, and Roy Hill. Sheryl's careful organization of countless records expedited my own research on the Huberts, and she generously shared Hubert family anecdotes and legends.

Great thanks go to Wanda Bobinger at the Polk County Historical Museum, who sent me a copy of Robert Wallace Hubert's diaries and two years later met to share information about the Huberts and Polk County history, and to Josh David, who gave the museum that copy of the diaries to begin with and without whom we never would have found the original location of Bob's, Jenny's, and Peggy's graves. Thanks to Josh for his sense of humor, historical know-how, and generosity, and for many helpful particulars ranging from names of Polk County trees to the joke I placed in Peggy's blue poem, "Lord, let us all go to heaven where there'll be no log train." Also in Polk County, thanks to Norma McLoughlin, whose local histories provided many essential details, and to Bernice Collins, who shared her memories of my great-grandmother Dinah Hubert Russell McKoy and her siblings. In Woodville, Texas, thanks to Carol Shields at the Whitemeyer Research Library and to Ofeira Gazzaway at the Heritage Museum. In Austin, thanks to Debbie Wise and Eric Beverly for being such generous hosts.

At the University of Pittsburgh in 2013-2014, thanks to Jeff Oaks, whose forms class paved the way for Peggy's blank-verse voice, to Terrance Hayes, who encouraged me to write the epistolary poem that starts off the book, and to Dawn Lundy Martin, who gave me the prompt that eventually became the book's overarching frame.

Great thanks to everyone at the Wisconsin Institute for Creative Writing. Without it this book might have remained an aspiration. I owe much, in particular, to Amaud Jamaul Johnson, who taught me how to organize my research in the early stages: Keep three notebooks—a notebook for images, a notebook for diction, a notebook for narrative facts.

I am also grateful for the extensive collection of the Wisconsin Historical Society, where I was able to find esoteric materials on nearly everything from Hood's Texas Brigade and the Georgia Military Institute to multiple volumes of the Federal Writers Project's Texas ex-slave narratives.

Also in Madison at the time, thanks to Erin Anthony, Kara Candito, Lewis Freedman, Amy Groshek, Lisa Hollenbach, Megan Milks, Katrina Schaag, Anna Vitale, Meg Wade, Tana Welch, and Timothy Welch: without your feedback, encouragement, and keen critical reading skills, this would have been a lesser work. Thanks especially to Lewis Freedman for our weekly writing sessions in Madison Sourdough, which kept me accountable to the project, and later for astute feedback on the full draft long after we had both moved to other cities. I am also indebted to Tana Welch, whose comments on the next-to-final draft resulted in a better ending for this book and made me consider how despite my best intentions I continue to perpetuate the very frameworks I am so intent on resisting. Thanks to Jordan Dunn for the painstaking limited-edition broadside of four pages from this work and for trekking to the Wisconsin Historical Society to make high-resolution scans of the page from Emma Haynes's *History of Polk County* after I had moved away. Cherod Johnson, thanks for insightful contributions to social media and for allowing me to quote from them.

Upon my return to Pittsburgh, thanks to the students in my Spring 2017 Readings in Contemporary Poetry class, whose ongoing discussion of time helped me think through the organization and materiality of this book. Also in the reconstituted Pittsburgh, thanks to Laura Brun, John Calvasina, Alicia Salvadeo, Leigh Thomas, and Chad Vogler for invaluable critiques, to Robert Bland for helpful reading recommendations, to Imani Owens for steadfast friendship, and to April Flynn for writing meet-ups that helped me keep one toe in the work through the summer of 2016. I am grateful to Ted Tarka at the University of Pittsburgh's Digital Research Lab for making a number of high-resolution scans on short notice; to Tom Bair for last-minute proofreading assistance; to Joel Coggins for the family tree redesign; and to Khirsten Scott, whose 2018 talk about her archival research on historically black colleges inspired me to add the page about Gildersleeve's photographs of Paul Quinn College. Great thanks to Peter Campbell, for writing with me on weekends for the final push in the spring of 2018, and especially for driving me to Gettysburg and retracing Hubert's approximate route on the battlefield with as much enthusiasm as my own and a far superior sense of direction.

Thanks to John Holway for responding to my emails about Jesse Hubbard, to Patricia Bernstein for answering my questions about Waco and the lynching of Jesse Washington, to Don Young at Johnson's Island Preservation Society, who replied to my queries about the prison camp, and to Christi Sullivan, Media/Communications Director for the Alabama-Coushatta Tribe of Texas, for fact-checking dates pertaining to the reservation. I am also indebted to John E. Nichols at Gettysburg National Military Park for his excellent tour of Little Round Top and for patiently answering my questions about the Fifth Texas Infantry's role in the attack.

At the National Archives in Washington, D.C., great thanks to Dennis Edelin, Bryan Cheeseboro, and citizen archivist Jonathan Deiss. Thanks to Dennis in particular for the magical afternoon I spent in the reading room with Robert Wallace Hubert's service records and for the high-resolution scan of the transfer record from Fort Delaware to Johnson's Island.

A good number of the poems in this book were forced into being over three successive Cave Canem retreats, a laboratory for what is possible when community meets the page. At Cave Canem, special thanks to Lyrae Van Clief-Stefanon, whose charge to think about black joy in history has formed an undercurrent for the book and kept me, I hope, from "buying into" narratives of abjection. Also thanks to an all-star faculty: Toi Derricotte, Cornelius Eady, Amber Flora Thomas, Chris Abani, Evie Shockley, Kevin Young, Ruth Ellen Kocher, Major Jackson, and Dawn Lundy Martin (again!). And to all my fellow fellows who workshopped versions of some of these poems: Aziza Barnes, Matthew Broaddus, Adrienne Christian, Jeremy Michael Clark, Sean DesVignes, Camonghne Felix, Raina Fields, Kadeem Gayle, Yalonda Green, Chinaka Hodge, Raven Jackson, Jaamil Kosoko, Nick Makoha, Nicholas Nichols, Ashunda Norris, Dustin Pearson, Kathy Z. Price, Maisha Quint, Aaron Samuels, Nicole Shanté, Chris Slaughter, April Walker, and Rashida Williams.

Thanks to the Millay Colony for the Arts for time and space to find my way back into the book after I had fallen out, and to my wonderful cohort there in July of 2017: Hui-Ying Tsai, Gemma Cooper-Novack, Judson Merrill, Harriet Clark, Amelia Evans, and especially Darryl Lauster, who generously helped me decipher Jesse Hubbard's baseball statistics. Also thanks to Douglas Rothschild in nearby Albany, for our conversations about Gettysburg that month. Thanks to VIDA for selecting me for a fellowship to the Home School in 2016 and to Tan Lin, whose workshop there rebooted my relationship to language and the source texts. I am also grateful to the Virginia Center for Creative Arts, where I went over the full manuscript in August of 2019 with an Afro pick followed by a fine-toothed comb.

Thank you to Sarah Stefana Smith for the cover art and for collaborating toward a future installation in conversation with *Descent*.

This project is supported in part by an award from the National Endowment for the Arts. In addition, great thanks to the Wisconsin Institute for Creative Writing at the University of Wisconsin-Madison and to the University of Pittsburgh for financial support for this work.

Thank you, finally, to Christian Peet and Elena Georgiou at Tarpaulin Sky Press, for making a home for hybrid books and for believing in this one. Thanks to Christian in particular for painstaking attention to the layout, treating this work with such great care.

ABOUT THE AUTHOR

Lauren Russell is the author of *What's Hanging on the Hush* (Ahsahta Press, 2017). A 2017 National Endowment for the Arts Creative Writing Fellow in Poetry, she has also received fellowships from Cave Canem, The Wisconsin Institute for Creative Writing, and VIDA/The Home School, and residencies from the Rose O'Neill Literary House at Washington College, the Millay Colony for the Arts, and City of Asylum/Passa Porta. Her work has appeared in *The New York Times Magazine*, the Academy of American Poets' *Poem-a-Day*, *boundary 2*, *The Brooklyn Rail*, *Cream City Review*, and the anthologies *Bettering American Poetry 2015* and *Furious Flower: Seeding the Future of African American Poetry*, among others. She is a research assistant professor in English and is assistant director of the Center for African American Poetry and Poetics at the University of Pittsburgh. Beginning in the fall of 2020, she will be assistant professor and director of the Center for Poetry at the Residential College in the Arts and Humanities at Michigan State University.

TARPAULIN SKY PRESS

exquisite imagination ... **(Publishers Weekly "Best Books 2018")** warped from one world to another **(The Nation)**; beautifully startling and fucked and funny and tender and sad and putrid and glitter-covered all at once. **(VICE)**; simultaneously metaphysical and visceral ... scary, sexual, intellectually disarming **(Huffington Post)**; only becomes more surreal **(NPR Books)**; proves indie presses deserve your attention **(BuzzFeed News)**; hallucinatory ... trance-inducing **(Publishers Weekly "Best Summer Reads")**; wholly new **(Iowa Review)**; language dissolves into stream-of-consanguinity post-surrealism and then resolves into a plot again **(Harriet, The Poetry Foundation)**; horrifying and humbling in their imaginative precision **(The Rumpus)**; a world of wounded voices **(Hyperallergic)**; riotous, rapturous, and radical **(LA Review of Books)**; unapologetic work, so bitch and bad-ass **(VIDA)**; Visceral Surrealism **(Fanzine)**; as savagely anti-idealist as Burroughs or Guyotat or Ballard **(Entropy)**; both devastating and uncomfortably enjoyable **(American Book Review)**; consistently inventive **(TriQuarterly)**; highly rewarding **(The Stranger)**; feels like coming **(Maudlin House)**; breakneck prose harnesses the throbbing pulse of language itself **(Publishers Weekly)**; an orgy ... at once sexy and scientifically compelling **(The Rumpus)**; dark, multivalent, genre-bending ... unrelenting, grotesque beauty (Publishers Weekly); futile, sad, and beautiful **(NewPages)**; refreshingly eccentric **(The Review of Contemporary Fiction)**; a kind of nut job's notebook **(Publishers Weekly)**; thought-provoking, inspired and unexpected. Highly recommended **(After Ellen)**

MORE FROM TS PRESS >>

REBECCA BROWN
NOT HEAVEN, SOMEWHERE ELSE

If heaven is somewhere, it isn't with us, but somewhere we want to get — a state, a place, a turning to home. Novel- and essayist Rebecca Brown's thirteenth book is narrative cycle that revamps old fairy tales, movies, and myths, as it leads the reader from darkness to light, from harshness to love, from where we are to where we might go.

PRAISE FOR *NOT HEAVEN, SOMEWHERE ELSE*: "Aside from 'genius,' the other word I would use to describe Rebecca Brown is 'elemental'…. She's a genius at the invisible forces that bind words together…. It feels dangerous and exciting, like if she puts her big brain to it long enough, she could completely rewrite the story of who we are." (PAUL CONSTANT, *SEATTLE REVIEW OF BOOKS*) "Satisfied a desire for moral discussion I didn't even know I had…. Highly recommended and highly rewarding." (RICH SMITH, *THE STRANGER*) PRAISE FOR REBECCA BROWN: "Strips her language of convention to lay bare the ferocious rituals of love and need." (*THE NEW YORK TIMES*) "One of the few truly original modern lesbian writers, one who constantly pushes both her own boundaries and those of her readers." (*SAN FRANCISCO CHRONICLE*) "Watch for her books and hunt down her short stories." (DOROTHY ALLISON) "America's only real rock 'n' roll schoolteacher." (THURSTON MOORE, SONIC YOUTH)

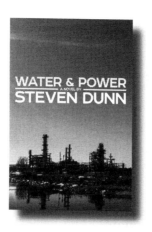

STEVEN DUNN
WATER & POWER

SPD Fiction Bestseller
Featured at *Buzzfeed News*:
"Books That Prove Indie Presses Deserve Your Attention"

Navy veteran Steven Dunn's second novel, *water & power,* plunges into military culture and engages with perceptions of heroism and terrorism. In this shifting landscape, deployments are feared, absurd bureaucracy is normalized, and service members are consecrated. *water & power* is a collage of voices, documents, and critical explorations that disrupt the usual frequency channels of military narratives. "Traversing both horror and humor, Dunn imbues his prose with the kind of duality that is hard to achieve, but pays off." (WENDY J. FOX, *BUZZFEED NEWS*) "Dunn's remarkable talent for storytelling collapses the boundaries between poetry and prose, memoir and fiction." (NIKKI WALLSCHLAEGER) "Captures the difficult, funny, abject, exhilarating, heartbreaking and maddening aspects of Navy life, both on and off duty. Read this book and understand the veterans in your life better, understand the aggressive disconnection the armed forces demands, and retain a much clearer picture of the people who wear the uniform in America's name." (KHADIJAH QUEEN)

JENNIFER S. CHENG
MOON: LETTERS, MAPS, POEMS

Co-winner, Tarpaulin Sky Book Award, chosen by Bhanu Kapil
Publishers Weekly, Starred Review
SPD Poetry Bestseller
Nominated for the PEN American Open Book Award

Mixing fable and fact, extraordinary and ordinary, Jennifer S. Cheng's hybrid collection, *Moon: Letters, Maps, Poems*, draws on various Chinese mythologies about women, particularly that of Chang'E (the Lady in the Moon), uncovering the shadow stories of our myths. "Exhilarating ... An alt-epic for the 21st century ... Visionary ... Rich and glorious." **(PUBLISHERS WEEKLY STARRED REVIEW)** "If reading is a form of pilgrimage, then Cheng gives us its charnel ground events, animal conversions, guiding figures and elemental life." **(BHANU KAPIL)** "Each of the voices in Jennifer S. Cheng's *Moon* speaks as if she's 'the last girl on earth.' ... With curiosity and attention, *Moon* shines its light on inquiry as art, asking as making. In the tradition of Fanny Howe's poetics of bewilderment, Cheng gives us a poetics of possibility." **(JENNIFER TSENG)** "Cheng's newest poetry collection bravely tests language and the beautiful boundaries of body and geography ... A rich and deeply satisfying read." **(AIMEE NEZHUKUMATATHIL)**

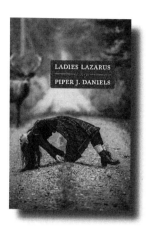

PIPER J. DANIELS
LADIES LAZARUS

Co-winner, Tarpaulin Sky Book Award
Nominated for the PEN/Diamonstein-Spielvogel Award
for the Art of the Essay

Equal parts séance, polemic, and love letter, Piper J. Daniels's *Ladies Lazarus* examines evangelical upbringing, sexual trauma, queer identity, and mental illness with a raw intensity that moves between venom and grace. Fueled by wanderlust, Daniels travels the country, unearthing the voices of forgotten women. Girls and ghosts speak freely, murdered women serve as mentors, and those who've languished in unmarked graves convert their names to psalms. At every turn, Daniels invites the reader to engage, not in the soothing narrative of healing, but in the literal and metaphorical dynamism of death and resurrection. "Beautifully written collection of 11 lyric essays ... Daniels emerges as an empowering and noteworthy voice." (*PUBLISHERS WEEKLY*) "*Ladies Lazarus* is the best debut I've read in a long time. Daniels has resurrected the personal essay and what it is and what it can do." (JENNY BOULLY) "An extremely intelligent, impressively understated, and achingly powerful work." (DAVID SHIELDS) "A siren song from planet woman, a love letter from the body, a resistance narrative against the dark." (LIDIA YUKNAVITCH)

STEVEN DUNN
POTTED MEAT

Co-winner, Tarpaulin Sky Book Award
Shortlist, *Granta*'s "Best of Young American Novelists"
Finalist, Colorado Book Award
SPD Fiction Bestseller

Set in a decaying town in West Virginia, Steven Dunn's debut novel, *Potted Meat*, follows a boy into adolescence as he struggles with abuse, poverty, alcoholism, and racial tensions. A meditation on trauma and the ways in which a person might surivive, if not thrive, *Potted Meat* examines the fear, power, and vulnerability of storytelling itself. "101 pages of miniature texts that keep tapping the nails in, over and over, while speaking as clearly and directly as you could ask.... Bone Thugs, underage drinking, alienation, death, love, Bob Ross, dreams of blood.... Flooded with power." (**BLAKE BUTLER**, *VICE MAGAZINE*) "Full of wonder and silence and beauty and strangeness and ugliness and sadness....This book needs to be read." (**LAIRD HUNT**) "A visceral intervention across the surface of language, simultaneously cutting to its depths, to change the world.... I feel grateful to be alive during the time in which Steven Dunn writes books." (**SELAH SATERSTROM**)

ELIZABETH HALL
I HAVE DEVOTED MY LIFE TO THE CLITORIS

Co-winner, Tarpaulin Sky Book Award
Finalist, Lambda Literary Award for Bisexual Nonfiction
SPD Nonfiction Bestseller

Debut author Elizabeth Hall set out to read everything that has been written about the clitoris. The result is "Freud, terra cotta cunts, hyenas, anatomists, and Acker, mixed with a certain slant of light on a windowsill and a leg thrown open invite us. Bawdy and beautiful." (**WENDY C. ORTIZ**). "An orgy of information ... rendered with graceful care, delivering in small bites an investigation of the clit that is simultaneously a meditation on the myriad ways in which smallness hides power." (***THE RUMPUS***) "Marvelously researched and sculpted.... bulleted points rat-tat-tatting the patriarchy, strobing with pleasure." (**DODIE BELLAMY**) "Philosophers and theorists have always asked what the body is—Hall just goes further than the classical ideal of the male body, beyond the woman as a vessel or victim, past genre as gender, to the clitoris. And we should follow her." (***KENYON REVIEW***) "Gorgeous little book about a gorgeous little organ.... The 'tender button' finally gets its due." (**JANET SARBANES**) "You will learn and laugh .... God this book is glorious." (**SUZANNE SCANLON**)

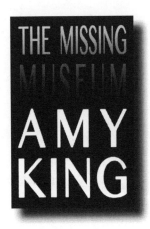

AMY KING
THE MISSING MUSEUM

Co-winner, Tarpaulin Sky Book Award
SPD Poetry Bestseller

Nothing that is complicated may ever be simplified, but rather catalogued, cherished, exposed. *The Missing Museum* spans art, physics & the spiritual, including poems that converse with the sublime and ethereal. They act through ekphrasis, apostrophe & alchemical conjuring. They amass, pile, and occasionally flatten as matter is beaten into text. Here is a kind of directory of the world as it rushes into extinction, in order to preserve and transform it at once. "'Understanding' is not a part of the book's project, but rather a condition that one must move through like a person hurriedly moving through a museum." (***PUBLISHERS WEEKLY***) "Women's National Book Association Award-winner Amy King balances passages that can prompt head-scratching wonder with a direct fusillade of shouty caps…. You're not just seeing through her eyes but, perhaps more importantly, breathing through her lungs." (***LAMBDA LITERARY***) "A visceral stunner … and an instruction manual…. King's archival work testifies to the power—however obscured by the daily noise of our historical moment—of art, of the possibility for artists to legislate the world." (***KENYON REVIEW***)

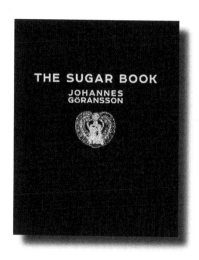

JOHANNES GÖRANSSON
THE SUGAR BOOK

SPD Poetry Bestseller

Johannes Göransson's *The Sugar Book* marks the author's third title with TS Press, following his acclaimed *Haute Surveillance* and *entrance to a colonial pageant in which we all begin to intricate.* "Doubling down on his trademark misanthropic imagery amid a pageantry of the unpleasant, Johannes Göransson strolls through a violent Los Angeles in this hybrid of prose and verse…. The motifs are plentiful and varied … pubic hair, Orpheus, law, pigs, disease, Francesca Woodman … and the speaker's hunger for cocaine and copulation….. Fans of Göransson's distorted poetics will find this a productive addition to his body of work". (**PUBLISHERS WEEKLY**) "Sends its message like a mail train. Visceral Surrealism. His end game is an exit wound." (**FANZINE**) "As savagely anti-idealist as Burroughs or Guyotat or Ballard. Like those writers, he has no interest in assuring the reader that she or he lives, along with the poet, on the right side of history." (**ENTROPY MAGAZINE**) "Convulses wildly like an animal that has eaten the poem's interior and exterior all together with silver." (**KIM HYESOON**) "'I make a language out of the bleed-through.' Göransson sure as fuck does. These poems made me cry. So sad and anxious and genius and glarey bright." (**REBECCA LOUDON**)

AARON APPS
INTERSEX

"Favorite Nonfiction of 2015," Dennis Cooper
SPD Bestseller and Staff Pick

Intersexed author Aaron Apps's hybrid-genre memoir adopts and upends historical descriptors of hermaphroditic bodies such as "imposter," "sexual pervert," "freak of nature," and "unfortunate monstrosity," tracing the author's own monstrous sex as it perversely intertwines with gender expectations and medical discourse. "Graphic vignettes involving live alligators, diarrhea in department store bathrooms, domesticity, dissected animals, and the medicalization of sex.... Unafraid of failure and therefore willing to employ risk as a model for confronting violence, living with it, learning from it." (**AMERICAN BOOK REVIEW**) "I felt this book in the middle of my own body. Like the best kind of memoir, Apps brings a reader close to an experience of life that is both 'unattainable' and attentive to 'what will emerge from things.' In doing so, he has written a book that bursts from its very frame." (**BHANU KAPIL**)

Excerpts from *Intersex* were nominated for a Pushcart Prize by *Carolina Quarterly*, and appear in *Best American Essays 2014*.

CLAIRE DONATO
BURIAL

A debut novella that slays even seasoned readers. Set in the mind of a narrator who is grieving the loss of her father, who conflates her hotel room with the morgue, and who encounters characters that may not exist, *Burial* is a little story about an immeasurable black hole; an elegy in prose at once lyrical and intelligent, with no small amount of rot and vomit and ghosts. "Poetic, trance-inducing language turns a reckoning with the confusion of mortality into readerly joy at the sensuality of living." (*PUBLISHERS WEEKLY* "BEST SUMMER READS") "A dark, multivalent, genre-bending book.... Unrelenting, grotesque beauty an exhaustive recursive obsession about the unburiability of the dead, and the incomprehensibility of death." (*PUBLISHERS WEEKLY* STARRED REVIEW) "Dense, potent language captures that sense of the unreal that, for a time, pulls people in mourning to feel closer to the dead than the living.... Sartlingly original and effective." (*MINNEAPOLIS STAR-TRIBUNE*) "A grief-dream, an attempt to un-sew pain from experience and to reveal it in language." (*HTML GIANT*) "A full and vibrant illustration of the restless turns of a mind undergoing trauma.... Donato makes and unmakes the world with words, and what is left shimmers with pain and delight." (BRIAN EVENSON) "A gorgeous fugue, an unforgettable progression, a telling I cannot shake." (HEATHER CHRISTLE) "Claire Donato's assured and poetic debut augurs a promising career." (BENJAMIN MOSER)

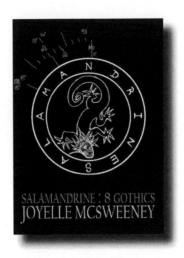

JOYELLE MCSWEENEY
SALAMANDRINE: 8 GOTHICS

Following poet and playwright Joyelle McSweeney's acclaimed novels *Flet*, from Fence Books, and *Nylund, The Sarcographer*, from Tarpaulin Sky Press, comes a collection of shorter prose texts by McSweeney, *Salamandrine: 8 Gothics*, perhaps better described as a series of formal/ generic lenses refracting the dread and isolation of contemporary life and producing a distorted, attenuated, spasmatic experience of time, as accompanies motherhood. "Vertiginous.... Denying the reader any orienting poles for the projected reality.... McSweeney's breakneck prose harnesses the throbbing pulse of language itself." (*PUBLISHERS WEEKLY*) "Biological, morbid, fanatic, surreal, McSweeney's impulses are to go to the rhetoric of the maternity mythos by evoking the spooky, sinuous syntaxes of the gothic and the cleverly constructed political allegory. At its core is the proposition that writing the mother-body is a viscid cage match with language and politics in a declining age.... This collection is the sexy teleological apocrypha of motherhood literature, a siren song for those mothers 'with no soul to photograph.'" (*THE BROOKLYN RAIL*) "Language commits incest with itself.... Sounds repeat, replicate, and mutate in her sentences, monstrous sentences of aural inbreeding and consangeous consonants, strung out and spinning like the dirtiest double-helix, dizzy with disease...." (*QUARTERLY WEST*)

JENNY BOULLY
*NOT MERELY BECAUSE OF THE UNKNOWN
THAT WAS STALKING TOWARD THEM*

"This is undoubtedly the contemporary re-treatment that Peter Pan deserves.... Simultaneously metaphysical and visceral, these addresses from Wendy to Peter in lyric prose are scary, sexual, and intellectually disarming." (*HUFFINGTON POST*) In her second SPD Bestseller from Tarpaulin Sky Press, *not merely because of the unknown that was stalking toward them*, Jenny Boully presents a "deliciously creepy" swan song from Wendy Darling to Peter Pan, as Boully reads between the lines of J. M. Barrie's *Peter and Wendy* and emerges with the darker underside, with sinister and subversive places. *not merely because of the unknown* explores, in dreamy and dark prose, how we love, how we pine away, and how we never stop loving and pining away. "To delve into Boully's work is to dive with faith from the plank — to jump, with hope and belief and a wish to see what the author has given us: a fresh, imaginative look at a tale as ageless as Peter himself." (*BOOKSLUT*) "Jenny Boully is a deeply weird writer— in the best way." (**ANDER MONSON**)

CHAPBOOKS

Sandy Florian, *32 Pedals and 47 Stops*
James Haug, *Scratch*
Claire Hero, *Dollyland*
Paula Koneazny, *Installation*
Paul McCormick, *The Exotic Moods of Les Baxter*
Teresa K. Miller, *Forever No Lo*
Jeanne Morel, *That Crossing Is Not Automatic*
Andrew Michael Roberts, *Give Up*
Brandon Shimoda, *The Inland Sea*
Chad Sweeney, *A Mirror to Shatter the Hammer*
Emily Toder, *Brushes With*

G.C. Waldrep, *One Way No Exit*

Tarpaulin Sky Literary Journal
in print and online

tarpaulinsky.com